'Chase draws on a lifetime of experience working with masks, and straddling the boundary line between theatre and therapy. His approach to mask through a theory of archetypes opens up rich possibilities in both domains. This book is both a practical guide and an eloquent manifesto.'
David Wiles, Professor of Drama, University of Exeter.

'Michael Chase's long experience as a mask maker and teacher provides a range of clear and thoughtful insights that will relax and disarm. He offers a layered range of exercises, in particular, ingenious ones to release the counter mask. This book opens the door to exciting, creative mask work!'
Gerry Flannigan, Artistic Director of Shifting Sands, and international mask and clown teacher, UK.

'I have found Mike Chase's temperament masks and exercises extremely helpful, to develop business management learners' capability for managing personality preferences when leading and working with others. This proved very useful at the University of Westminster Business School, and I continue to draw on the rich resources shared in this book for facilitating learning in my current activities.'
Andy Peisley, Senior Lecturer, Falmouth University.

'For anyone considering the relationship between fine art, theatre and therapy, this book gives an insight into the work of Michael Chase and The Mask Studio. Michael shares with us his world of 'The Mask' from the points of view of a sculptor, an applied theatre producer and most pertinently as a applied theatre practitioner. This is a timely publication, as so many theatre practitioners are now looking to transfer their skills to new areas of practice. The key to this book is its combination of Michael's experience of both making and using.'
Stephen Jon, artist, mask maker and lecturer in mask at Nottingham Trent University.

'Mike and I have been running clown and mask workshops for the last 8 years. Mask work allows actors to explore their connection to archetypal forces, myths, stories and images that profoundly inform the clown's presence on stage. These are skills which the actor-clown needs especially when working as modern day court jesters – reflecting back to society what is really going on. This book invites the reader on a journey of discovery and self-discovery through the mask.'
Vivian Gladwell, founder and director of Nose to Nose, clown workshops.

'This is a generous book, full of clear guidance and practical wisdom. Mike Chase brings to his authorship of this book his unique combination of experience and training as an actor, director, teacher, artist, mask maker and registered psychodrama psychotherapist. This book combines theatre history, the history of the use of mask, an account of the development of the idea of the four temperaments, and a highly detailed, step-by-step guide to mask making. Further, the book also explains tried and tested warm-up and group building activities and exercises to develop the skills of performing in mask, and describes the uses of mask in therapy, in schools, in teacher training, and in organisational and community development. I was particularly fascinated to read Chase's insights into how the masks based on the four temperaments can help in understanding emotion and promoting psychological integration, developmental repair and recovery from trauma.'

Clark Baim, Senior Trainer in Psychodrama Psychotherapy and founding Director of Geese Theatre UK.

'Mike Chase has written a much-welcomed book for educators and mask practitioners. I have used his four temperaments masks in many different educational and corporate settings in diverse countries from India to South Africa and Israel. Whether working with company managers seeking how to improve their team work or teachers in training preparing to enter the classroom or young people taking part in Leadership and Self Development courses, I have found the masks to be an extremely effective tool for embodying these four constitutional archetypes in a way which dynamically brings home their essential characters. They never fail to have a profound and illuminating effect on those seeking to know themselves better and to live more harmoniously with their fellow human beings. And they do so with both poignancy and humour. Over the years, these four masks have become my constant companions, and I am delighted to at last have a magnificent, detailed and above all practice-oriented book to substantiate, guide and inspire my use of mask in my educational work.'

Adrian Locher, Director, ASHA Centre.

MASK
Making, Using and Performing

Published by Hawthorn Press, Hawthorn House,
1 Lansdown Lane, Stroud, Gloucestershire, GL5 1BJ, UK
Tel: (01453) 757040 E-mail: info@hawthornpress.com

Hawthorn Press
www.hawthornpress.com

Illustrations by Allmut ffrench
Photography by Louise Stoner and Jane Chase
Design by Lucy Guenot
Printed by Melita Press, Malta

Extract from *The Temple* reproduced by kind permission of Peter Oswald.

Printed on environmentally friendly chlorine-free paper sourced from renewable forest stock.

British Library Cataloguing in Publication Data applied for
ISBN 978-1-907359-66-8

MASK
Making, Using and Performing

Mike Chase

Inspired by the four temperaments, for use in workshops, performance and therapy

Foreword by John Wright

Hawthorn Press

This book is dedicated to Rubin, Lia and Phoebe

ABOUT THE AUTHOR

Mike Chase has developed mask, mime and voice through an eclectic international education. He has taught and directed physical theatre, mime and mask at drama colleges and universities for over thirty years. He established the Mask Studio in the mid-nineties to develop masks for training, education, performance and therapy, which are used internationally by theatres and theatre companies including the RSC, the National Theatre, LAMDA, Trestle Theatre, Welsh National Opera and Told by an Idiot. He was the artistic director of the Glasshouse Art Centre for fifteen years where he developed the application of masks in *Hero's Journey*, a therapeutic programme for young adults with complex needs. Mike is presently working as a psychodrama psychotherapist in a high-security democratic therapeutic prison with violent offenders, using masks and psychodrama. He holds a master's degree in educational research and runs mask making and using workshops internationally.

ACKNOWLEDGEMENTS

This book is the result of many years of working with a number of intensely creative artist and therapists who literally changed my life and give rise to this work.

First and foremost John Wright for his tenacious and creative spirit and the years of collaboration, long may it continue. Manfred van Doorn for his interactive body work and adventurous explorations into the psychology of body soul and spirit. Aonghus Gordon for giving some of this work a home in the Ruskin Mill Trust, and all my fellow teachers, tutors and therapists who collaborated over many years. I would also like to acknowledge fellow mask makers, teachers and collaborators Ninnian Kinnier-Wilson and Denato Sartori, and further practitioners who have supported the writing of this book including Stephen Jon, Steven Winnery and Sally Brooks. Allmut ffrench has been a great exponent of this work over the years, and gave very generously of her time and talents to illustrate this book. And many of the great mask companies we have made masks for including Trestle Theatre Co, Moving Picture Mime Show, The Rose Theatre, Offaboom, Unfortunati, Kepow, Propeller Theatre Company and The Gambolling Guisers.

Finally my family who have all been part of this book, and helped realise it in so many seen and unseen ways, Jane, Rubin, Lia and Phoebe.

Cane is visited in the centre of the earth by the smith and the master builder, Hiram.

Cane: Hiram you have been here before. Whenever
You stand among the elements, the fire
Bright in the forge, the air, pumped from the bellows,
The earth, that is the red iron, and the water
That cools it black – whenever, at the centre
Of these four elements you stand, transported
Out of yourself, and your wild thoughts, the windlifted
Leaves of your mind, fall still, and for a moment
You are your work, then you are at the centre
Of the metallic planet, where we are,
Forever changing spirit into matter.

From *The Temple* by Peter Oswald, 2008

CONTENTS

FOREWORD

I first met Mike in the early eighties on one of my first mask workshops in London. I thought he was an actor. It wasn't until the end of the course that he told me he was a mask maker as well.

But I soon learnt how good a maker he was. Mike made many of the masks I still use today. He made the vast majority of my half-masks and all my naive masks and we've collaborated on numerous productions and projects since then. I feel I'm in safe hands when I commission a mask from Mike, and reading *Mask: Using, Making and Performing* only re-confirms that confidence.

Mask work is the place where sculpture and acting meet, and Mike's skills embrace both these topics. The care he takes over each process, his diligence as a teacher and his eye for three-dimensional shapes come across very clearly in his writing.

I've learnt a lot from Mike and we both learned a lot from Alit, the mask maker we both worked with in Bali. His influence focused our attention on the relationship between design and function in making masks. 'How do you want the mask to move?' Alit once asked me when I was trying to place a commission. It was a completely new idea to me that I should know this before the mask was made. Mike took it in his stride and today it's a well-established principal in his work. But in a culture like ours, with no established masked theatre tradition, ideas and reference for new masks have to be found.

In a making and using workshop that we ran together some years ago he produced, in our first session, two buckets; one containing slips of paper with various nouns such as 'baker', 'nurse' or 'wrestler' written on them, and the other with verbs such as 'lazy', 'randy', or 'sensitive'. The game was for everyone to take a slip of paper from each bucket so you might end up with a 'lazy nurse' or a 'sensitive wrestler' or 'randy baker'. The idea was to give you diverse elements to play with in the design of your mask.

Random clashes and pairings like these encourage you to come up with a face that's more subtle and more ambiguous than a simple recognisable type. As happens in life, an apparently crude combination of elements gives you a face that's capable of reflecting an astonishing range of feelings. The 'aggressive man' is just 'aggressive' but the 'sensitive wrestler' gives you a face that implies so much more.

This subtlety is a vital aspect of mask design but Mike presented it as a simple game for everyone to experience for themselves. There was no explanation or justification. We didn't need one; the work spoke for itself. You learn through 'doing' with Mike and this is the quality that comes out when you read his book.

John Wright

John is co-founder of Trestle Theatre Co and co-founder of Told by an Idiot. John is an international teacher of theatre. His book *Why Is That So Funny?* has gained popularity all over the world. His new book is *Playing the Mask: Acting Without Bullshit*, looking at what mask work can teach us about acting.

INTRODUCTION

Ever since I can remember, I have been interested in faces. At fourteen years old, in a boarding school in the mountains of South Africa, I began drawing faces. These were not the faces that I saw around me; rather they were faces of an inner world. Some were immensely distorted, expressing feelings that I was unable to voice in any other way; other faces were of a more supportive nature. These were feelings that perhaps most adolescents experience. Others however were more particular to me. Rudolf Steiner describes how adolescence is like an illness: it is an illness of the soul in which the individual is looking for himself in the myriad mirrors that life offers (Steiner, 2009, p 189). With young adults who are striving to make meaning out of the illness of adolescence, faces can be drawn and later transformed into masks. The outside of the mask becomes the externalized expression of an inner state, boiled down to its essence, arriving at an archetype that also has meaning for others. Filling the mask from the inside with the expression and breath, the body and gestures of the heightened state of the wearer open a doorway into another world. This vast and awe-inspiring world, both beautiful and terrifying, can be managed, named and expressed through the container of the mask.

As an educator and psychotherapist I have met many of these faces in the young adults with complex needs who have frequented the mask studio, drama room and psychodrama space. I have also encountered them amongst the groups of violent offenders volunteering for therapy in a high-security prison.

In the context of the theatre I have used masks to enhance theatrical performance by going beyond the style of psychological realism and into the realm of folk types, archetypes and spontaneous improvised theatre. I have also used different masks to teach drama students a number of distinct performance skills. Inspired by the mask-training practices of Jacques Lecoq, I have used a range of different styles, such as: the neutral mask, used for stripping down the actor to his or her bare essential self; the naive mask, used for exploring restrictive play; and the half masks from the Italian folk types of the *commedia dell'arte*. Working with Greek tragedy, I have developed a style of acoustic mask, inspired by Thanos Vovolis, to explore chorus work, vertical attention to the gods, and white-hot emotion. Whether the mask is used in performance, where the body language of the masked actor is under a microscope, or in training the actor to be more alive, spontaneous and focused, there is one common denominator: managing the paradox of having to be in touch with both our core creative impulses and the discipline of the stage.

The mask, by its very nature being a hard-and-fast expression of a given state, character or archetype, enables the user to explore what is captured in the mask without distraction. Whether this is in the theatre with a character upon the stage; for training actors in the rhythm and development of character; or for education of the teacher in managing themselves and the classroom, the mask can offer insight and experience. The application of masks in the field of therapy as a transitional object can enable the client to deal with powerful complex roles, bringing understanding and catharsis. These applications of the mask outside the art form suggest the notion of 'applied mask'. This book focuses on both the areas where mask can expand the possibilities of theatre, but can also be used as a tool for applied mask to enliven education, consulting in organisations and therapy.

How to read this book

This book is developed as a whole and yet can be used effectively in its parts to research questions and support practice in a number of different fields. It can be read cover to cover; but it could also be of benefit to focus on specific questions. The chapters on the general making and using of masks remain outside of the theme of the temperaments, and offer a basic approach to the making and use of masks. The different focuses of projects for face casting, the four temperaments and the neutral offer a holistic approach to the overall theme. However a specific focus might well be all that is required to answer the questions of how to apply a mask in a specific context, where any one of the six projects could be of value. The applications of the work in different fields offer a broad range of topics, from educating teachers, to training actors, working in schools, theatre companies, consulting in organisations, social communities and application in therapy. These build on some of the previous exercises and can be easily used with specific interests and practices.

This book is in four sections. The first is looking at the background to masks and the temperaments. The second focuses on mask making, begins generally, then becomes more specific with each of the temperaments. The third section looks at mask using, considering first a general approach, becoming more specific to the four temperaments. The fourth section looks at the application of this work across a wide spectrum of mask-using practice.

Chapter I

THE BACKGROUND

For mask makers in the modern western world there is a frighteningly blank canvas in comparison to the mask traditions of Bali, Japan, West Africa, Native America and the many other Eastern traditions of mask making and using. Traditional mask makers from antiquity worked continually from the question: what is required from the mask for the preservation of society? Another way to ask this question could be: what gods do we need to embody in order to restore balance in the world? Masks and mask makers and users had an important role in these traditional societies not only as healers but also as storytellers. Masks helped the dancer priests with the embodiment of the characters, spirits and gods from the stories, which would guide the ethical choices and moral development of society. Performers in ancient Greece used masks in their religious ceremonies for the enactment of mythology. Even though images and sculptures of these masks survive, they have not been taken up by western society as a lineage of mask traditions. The vivid vocabulary of masks from the Italian *commedia dell'arte* do offer the western mask maker a tradition to draw on. However, as the masks are grotesque and animal in design, and refer predominantly to a comic style, their reference is limited to the nuances and complexities of modern life.

This has led to the struggle for the western mask maker to understand and penetrate the practice of mask making with any lawfulness. The subjective notions of practitioners' reliance on fantasy usually leads to masks which are either sentimental or grotesque. Theatre director Peter Brook (1993) challenges the use of masks in western theatre, describing them in two ways: there is a mask that is life giving, which affects

Commedia dell'arte masks

Rangda witch mask from Bali by Ida Bagus

the wearer and the observer in a very positive way; and there is another, which distorts the wearer, creating a distorted reality for the observer.

Brook's argument lies with the mask makers, who, in the western world, have no continuous tradition in mask making, but rely on subjective psychological masks, which might be better used in the therapeutic arena, as an expression of parts of the psyche rather than for use on the stage. This conundrum has led me to seek out meaningful cosmologies, ordered wholes, on which to develop my practice as a mask maker. Over the past thirty years the temperaments and other archetypes, including the seven planets and the zodiac, have been the foundation stones for my mask designs. They have helped a process of understanding the human condition in psychological terms but also in supporting the responsibility I have as a mask maker.

Mask using in the western tradition

According to Aristotle, theatre originated when Thespis, the Greek actor, who, instead of singing in the chorus, took a bold step and performed as a principle actor by transforming himself from one character to another through the use of masks. This act, which took place around sixth century BC could well be considered the beginning of theatre as we know it today, and may have been the first use of masks for the theatre outside of ritual. Actors with masks are depicted on Greek vases, holding masks before going onto the stage. From this time there was a gradual change in the performances from the plays of the ancient myths of Demeter and Persephone (Schuré, 1936), to ancient mythology characterised by Homer and dramatised by the great tragedians Aeschylus, Sophocles and Euripides.

In the fourteenth century in Italy, following a period of change from the Christian mystery plays, the *commedia dell'arte* came into being, a secular performance style expressing human experience rather than religious stories. The masks for the *commedia*, some of which have survived, were made of leather. It is interesting to note that at the time of the *commedia* (1500s to 1700s), the Topeng masks of Bali were being developed for a dance that celebrated the human being, as opposed to the gods and spirits of Bali. The folk characters of both Bali and the Italian *commedia* players depicted recognisable, national social types.

Between the sixteenth century and the nineteenth century the mask died in Europe (Rudlin, 1994) and was picked up again by Jacques Copeau in France in 1920s. Copeau was interested in the capacity of the mask to 'command' the actor in character development, bodily gesture, movement, voice and speech. Copeau observed that it is not only the actor's face that is altered by being in a mask, but also the nature of his reflexes and feelings, which would have been unimaginable had his face been uncovered (Cole and Chinoy, 1970). Copeau wanted his actors to be taken over by the mask and to enter into a marriage with it.

An inspiration to three generations of mask makers, actors and teachers, Copeau sparked an entire renaissance of mask work in Europe. Saint Denis, Devine, Le Coq, Johnston, Brook, Grotowski and Wright took up the mask and developed performance and acting training, which has sparked some of the most inspiring theatre companies, including Complicité, Moving Picture Mime Show and Trestle, to name a few (Ives, 1996). This was as if in response to Edward Gordon Craig, who insisted that the mask is that paramount means of dramatic expression without which acting was bound to degenerate (Craig, 1919).

One might ask why masks have such a dramatic effect upon both performer and audience. Cyril Ives suggests that the work of the mask is to serve as an intentional object which, through the language of symbol and ritual, connects the body to the cosmos or the wider universe (Ives, 1996, p 35). As a symbolic transformation of the face, the mask draws and centres the gaze of both actors and audience.

Masks in therapy

The application of masks in healing has been used for thousands of years, from the Bhutanese and Sinhalese mask dances to ward off evil spirits, to the Korean mask dances to overcome disease. The contemporary western application of masks in therapy is, as in the use of masks in theatre, recent and scant. A handful of psychologists, psychiatrists and psychotherapists have made it their mission to research the use of masks in therapy for clients with differing needs.

The main contributions to the literature and research into masks in therapy are from Sue Jennings, the founder of Dramatherapy in the UK, and Robert Landy. And yet, as mask researcher Cyril Ives points out, there seems to be little comment within psychotherapy as a whole to the development of this area of practice. The little that there is focuses predominantly on the making of masks, and less on the use and embodiment of the mask. Some interesting observations on the therapeutic use of masks include their role in developing 'psychological vigour', through the spontaneity the mask engenders when it is worn; revealing an 'archetypal truth', through the concretisation of specific images and features; living through deep content in a 'controlled fashion', through the focused representation of the masks which can be put on and taken off at will; and the mask's role in working with 'parts of self', through the concrete representation of different feelings, thoughts and intentions. These psychological terms and references are significant for the work intended here, as a reminder that even though this is not an exposition of masks in therapy, the masks cannot help but be therapeutic. Ultimately the mask is a powerful catalyst for experiencing dynamic forces within the realm of body and imagination, or, as will be referred to later, as the imaginative body.

So why use temperaments – what can they offer the mask? Put another way, what can masks offer in helping to understand the temperaments, what they are and how they affect us?

The four temperaments and their uses

Since the mid 1980s, ever since I attended a workshop at the Novalis Centre in Cape Town, I have had something to do with the temperaments most weeks. What captured my attention was the simplicity and depth of this cosmology and the manner by which it is applicable in all walks of life. This can be a tool to understand the self, relationships and behaviour, managing a classroom, training actors for the stage, mask makers for the theatre and design, mask using as a professional development process in education, business, therapy and theatre performance. Whether emphasising the four elements or the four directions, the four temperaments have been taken up contemporaneously in many ways. Analytic psychologist C G Jung developed a theory of personality types very akin to the four temperaments, which were taken further by Katharine Cook-Briggs and her daughter Isabel Briggs Myers in the Myers-Briggs Type Indicator (Kiersey, 1943). Actor, director and acting teacher Michael Chekhov developed exercises inspired by the four temperaments which he called the 'Four Brothers of Art', including ease, form beauty and wholeness. (Chekhov, 1991)

In order to understand the origin of the temperaments we need to go back to the pre-Socratic Greek philosopher Empedocles (c. 492–432 BC). In meditating upon the known physical universe, Empedocles observed that all physical substance can be understood through four basic categories, which he called the four elements. All physical substance is comprised of earth, water, fire and air, or any number of combinations of them. Of all the ninety-eight elements in the Periodic Table, all can be resolved down to the four basic elements of earth, water, fire or air. Empedocles was a great influence on Aristotle's understanding of the known universe.

Ancient Greek and Latin writing ascribed to Hermes Trismegistus suggested that 'if all the four elements are combined together in fit proportions, then the creature is so made as to be ardent in action, light of movement ... and solid in structure. For the earthy element is that which makes the body solid; the watery element is that in it which makes it diffuse itself so as to unite with things; the airy element is that in us which causes movement; and all these are roused to action by the fire in us.' (Scott, 1924)

It was the work of Empedocles that created the ground for Hippocrates (born c. 460 BC) and the development of the four humours, which became the basis for medicine up until the nineteenth century. The use of the four humours in medicine was taken up by physicians in Persia and Egypt, as well as in India, with the three humours of the Ayurveda and the five humours of the Hindu tradition.

This was to lay the foundation for Hildegard of Bingen (born 1098) to build her understanding of the 'correspondences'. Hildegard, a Benedictine abbess living on the Rhine in Germany developed the idea that what is out in the cosmos (the macrocosm) has correspondence within the human being (the microcosm). This principle

– 'as above, so below' – can also be seen as what is outside in the world is also within the human being. That the four elements exist within the physical make-up of the human being is perhaps easy to grasp; taking that a step further, using the philosophy of Hildegard, we might conclude that these elements had correspondences within the human body and soul.

Austrian philosopher and pedagogue Rudolf Steiner (1861–1925), the founder of anthroposophy and spiritual science, took up Hippocrates' work on the four humours and Hildegard's work on correspondences and developed a rich theory arising from his research into the science of the spirit.

Steiner describes the human being as four fold. He posits that the physical body, the densest part of which is the bones and skeletal system, arises out of the mineral world, having its connection to the physical earth. What distinguishes the plant from the mineral is that the plant has life. Steiner describes how the human being, like a plant, has a life body, or 'etheric body', which keeps the physical body alive, having its connection to the element of water of which over seventy per cent of the human body is comprised. The third aspect of the human being is a body of feelings, instincts and desires, which Steiner describes as the 'astral body', residing in the nervous system. The astral body, which the human being has in common with animals, manifests in the animal in the capacity of fight, flight or freeze. The astral body, with its lightning capacity to pass information along the nervous system, has its connection to the air. What the human being has over and above the physical body (which we share with mineral world), an etheric body (which we share with plants), and an astral body (which we share with animals) is our ego. This ego, or 'I', is that part of the human being which enable us to physically stand upright, speak of one's self as an 'I', have more choices than the basic instincts of fight, flight and freeze and take hold of our destiny in the world. (Steiner, 2008)

How then do the temperaments arise, one might ask? Steiner posits the idea that the four temperaments arise out of the meeting between the hereditary stream through ancestral generations and an 'eternal individuality', coming from the spiritual world. It is generally taken for granted today that we inherit traits from our ancestors through the genetic inheritance of different features and abilities; however, it is not scientifically proven that there is a spiritual core of the human being that lives on after death of the physical body, except in various religions and doctrines about the spiritual world. Steiner is referring to his spiritual research arising out of spiritual science, elements of which are maintained in various religions, including Buddhism and Hinduism – that an eternal spiritual aspect exists for every human being. It is in this place – where what is physically inherited meets with our spiritual uniqueness – that temperament arises. The temperaments are the language and psychology mediating between the physical body and the psyche or soul. It is important to emphasise that the temperaments are not a medical model for treating the physical body, nor are they a psychological model for understanding the complexities of the thoughts, feelings and intentions that comprise the soul, but rather the connection of the physical body to the soul.

If we observe human nature it is possible to notice the following: when any one of the four elements comes to the fore and dominates, the temperament arises. When the physical body with the element of earth dominates, the human constitution of the melancholic temperament stands out. When the etheric forces of the element of water dominate, the phlegmatic temperament arises. The sanguine temperament connecting to the air element comes to the fore when the astral body and nervous system dominate; and the choleric temperament connected to the element of fire arises when the ego forces dominate.

Taking this a stage deeper, let us consider the following. In observing the human being as we go about our daily activities, we are not all the same, rather we have extraordinary differences, all of which make up the richness of variety in the human being. Some of us are tall, while others are more stocky, some of us are rounder, while others are more trim, light and bouncy. It is as if we can observe an archetype. Irrespective of culture, age, gender or disability, various tendencies can be observed. For example, one can often observe tall and thin people who are deep thinkers, who have a sensitive interest in the past, and feel the pain of the world most deeply. Here we get the feeling that these people have a predominance in their skeleton, where the gravity of earth seems to pull down more strongly. There can be a tendency for melancholics to feel the knocks of life so intensely that it is as if they are having to continually overcome their physical body.

Another person may be of a quiet and calm demeanour, never rushing or taking risks. These people may be slow and graceful, having a resistance to change. This is when the phlegmatic temperament might be dominating, revealing a vulnerability to being pushed, as if they are wading through a still pool, where you can't rush, because there is more resistance than only the thin air. Living in the here and now, in touch with their own feeling for life, the phlegmatic person is happier following on behind.

And yet a third person might feel everything in life very acutely, but instead of taking everything into themselves they respond to it all in the here and now, but in a light and airy manner. As if being blown by the breeze, the Sanguine continually responds to external stimuli and is always on the move. Any tragedy would be short lived. The Sanguine can be superficial and always on the periphery of life, yet the centre of the party. The Sanguine is often considered the temperament of childhood, which in an adult can reveal itself in a playful and light-hearted manner.

A fourth might feel very different from the preceding three, who might frustrate them no end. With passion and fire burning in their hearts, the choleric person is striving towards the future, leading from the top to a predetermined goal. Charismatic and determined though the Choleric can be, they can also be darn right hot and angry as they pursue their goals toward the future. Violence and destruction can be their part if the Choleric does not get their way. However, maturation brings the noble countenance of a powerful and kind leader, where egoism has been tempered, and the higher self comes to the fore in the service of others.

The four temperaments are an ordered whole offering on the one hand a cosmology that could benefit the making and using of masks, as they offer such clear descriptions of human nature. On the other hand, the activity of creating and using masks offers many opportunities to gain practical insights about the temperaments outside of a theoretical framework. The human body architecture, gesture and rhythm are clearly differentiated in the one-sidedness of each temperament. It is not surprising that the use of masks in working with a practical psychology for understanding the nature and differentiation of human beings could be very useful.

Chapter 2

GENERAL MASK MAKING

There are numerous methods of making masks and the scope of this book can only cover some of them. The concepts and techniques outlined below are not new. Some of them are standard sculpting techniques for design and casting, which I have simplified and adapted to the process of mask making. The section on the methods and choices of mask making materials are specific to mask construction.

None of the instructions in this book must be taken too rigidly, but rather as guidelines and suggestions gathered over the years by trial and error to aid to your own process of mask making. The processes that follow can be applied to the five projects, one for each of the temperaments and the neutral.

I would advise anyone starting out to face cast another willing person, rather than starting on oneself – and the following instructions are written with this in mind.

Face casting

In order to create masks that fit the user well (if not perfectly) finding the correct proportions of the user's face is necessary. The most effective way of achieving this is to face cast the person for whom the mask is being made, and then design the mask on top of the cast. The following method facilitates the creation of a mould from which a cast can be taken, upon which the mask can then be designed with exact proportions. Firstly you will make a face cast of the subject with plaster bandage and then cast in solid plaster.

Plaster bandage, also known as 'mod rock', can be used very effectively to make a negative cast of a person's face, which, once cast in plaster, results in a positive life-size cast. The person whose face is being cast *must* remain still for twenty minutes, and be prepared to undergo different experiences, which have variously been described as, 'meditative', 'challenging', 'claustrophobic', and 'amusing'.

Face-casting materials

- Bowl of tepid warm water
- Scissors
- Large spoon
- Pallet knife
- Sponge
- 100g dried terracotta clay
- Plaster bandage – 6 x 8' (2m x 20cm) is usually enough for a single face cast
- 2 kg plaster powder
- Vaseline or petroleum jelly
- Rubber cup 4" high
- Plastic modelling tool
- Washing-up liquid

Face-casting process

Working in pairs: face casting each other

The person being face cast needs to sit upright in a relaxed position on a comfortable chair. Their head is best covered in a cloth or swimming cap with all the hair tucked up inside. The surface of the face, from hairline to neck line, ear to ear, needs to be covered in Vaseline or petroleum jelly, covering thickly over areas where there is a lot of hair, i.e. eyebrows, eyelashes and beards.

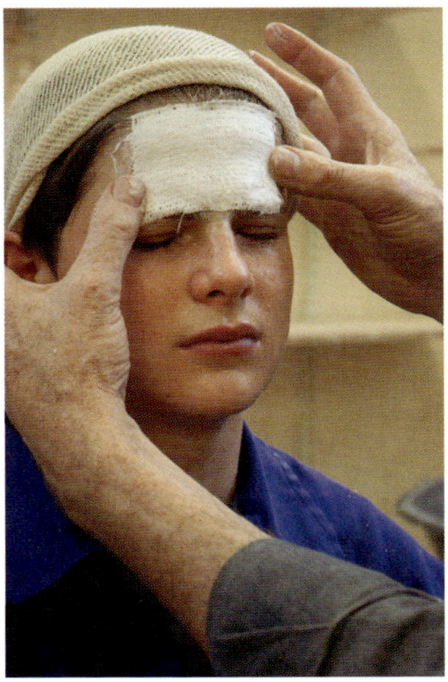

Prepare the plaster bandage, by cutting it up into strips in three sizes roughly to the following dimensions: 5 x 3" (12 x 8 cm), 4 x 2" (10 x 5 cm) and 2 x 1" (5 x 2.5 cm).

Dip the plaster bandage into the bowl of tepid water and lightly wipe it to get rid of any drips. Starting from the hair line, lay the plaster flat on the forehead and rub gently to smooth over the plaster (which is contained in the bandage), filling any holes that show through in the bandage. The bandage needs to be taken up to the beginning of the ear, and down under the chin up to the point where the neck starts, about 1.5" (4 cm) from the top.

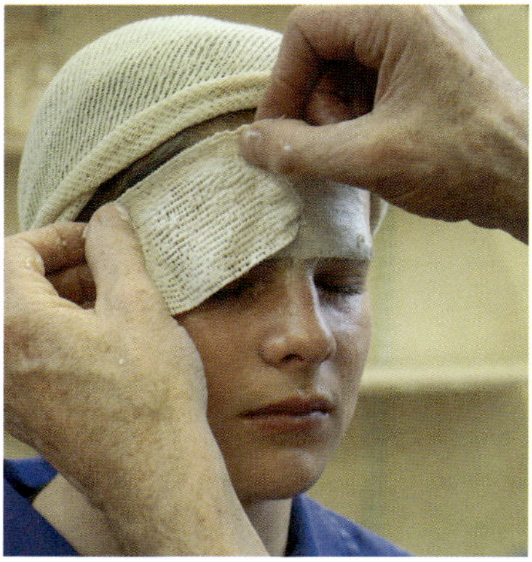

Repeat this process, overlapping each previously placed piece of bandage by at least half an inch (1 cm), and work in the second piece. Keep adding more pieces of plaster bandage until the whole of the face is covered, including the lips and mouth, leaving the two nostrils exposed for breathing. It is important to work each piece of bandage well into the other piece, and against the skin as this is what picks up the detail of the face, smoothed out.

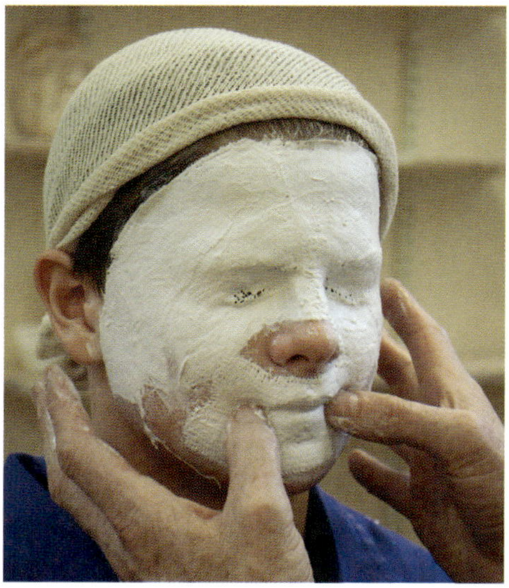

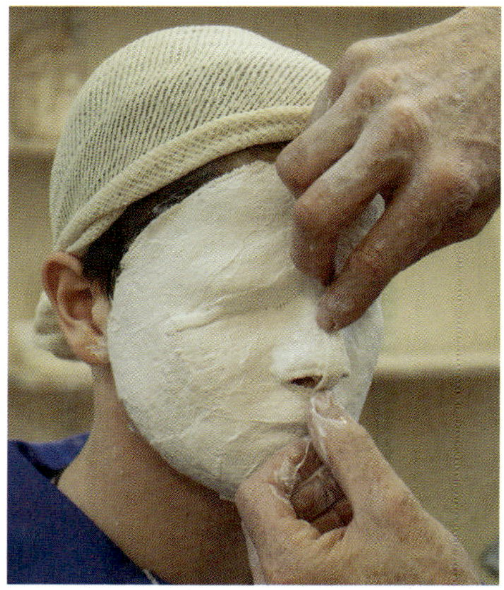

At the same time, use the smaller pieces of plaster bandage to go over the outside of the nostrils and between them. Take care not to take the bandage inside the nostril, but only up to the rim. Cover the ridge between the nostrils by running a thin folded strip about 2 inches long, from the tip of the nose, under and onto the top area of the lip. Cover the eyes last, so the person being face cast can see for as long as possible.

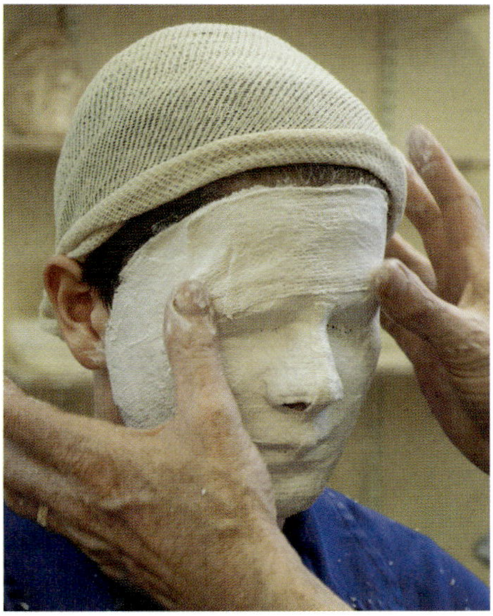

This whole process is then repeated with a second layer of bandage. During the second layering, reinforce the edges of the face cast by doubling the bandage (folding) and ensuring its folded edge lies flush with the first layer underneath around the outer edge.

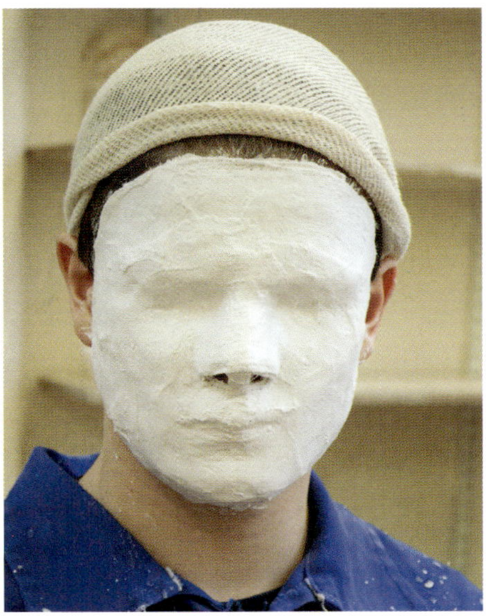

These layers are left to dry, which will take not much more than 10 minutes. Once the outer surface is dry, the person underneath the plaster can begin to move their face around by blowing lightly through their lips in order to move away the mould from their face, to try frowning, smiling etc, in order to loosen the plaster.

I suggest the person casting gives a running commentary of what they are doing to reassure the person being face cast that they are being cared for during the encounter.

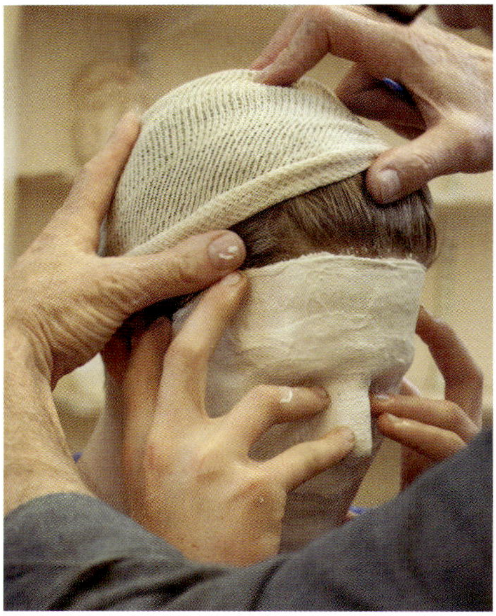
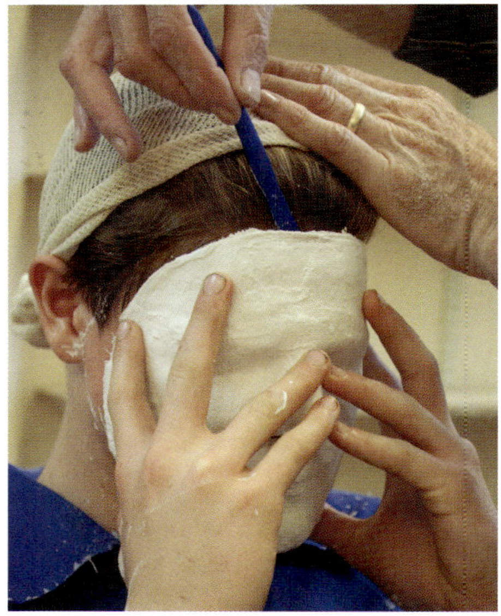

The mould should now be able to be lifted entirely off the face. If the mould sticks to the hair, use a modelling tool to free up the hair and remove the face cast.

At this point, the person being face cast may be quite relieved that the process is over and will be keen to have their face cleaned up. Offer them a clean towel, and then lead them to the bathroom or facility where they can wash and clean up their face.

This process creates a negative mould, which is half of the face-casting process. If you are working with a group this is the time where the casters and sitters can swap over and the process can be done again.

Preparing the mould

Once the mould has come off the face it will need to be reinforced. This is done by holding it up to a light, where the thinner areas will show which areas you need to attend to. Apply extra bandage to the outside of the negative mould. The nostrils will also need to be filled, with a small folded piece of bandage, laid on the outside and pushed lightly up the nostril hole to create the indentation of the nostril.

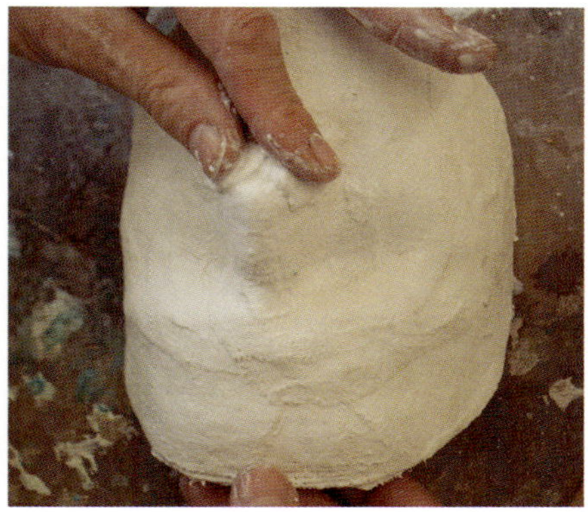

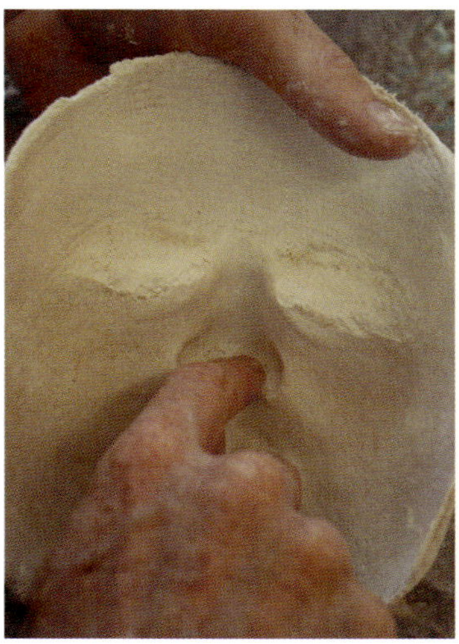

If there are any rough pieces of plaster bandage sticking up, trim them off the outer edge with a pair of scissors.

Then brush the mould on the inside with 1:1 part solution of petroleum jelly and washing-up liquid. This acts as a release agent to the solid plaster that will follow. It also needs to be painted on the rim and about an inch around the outside layer.

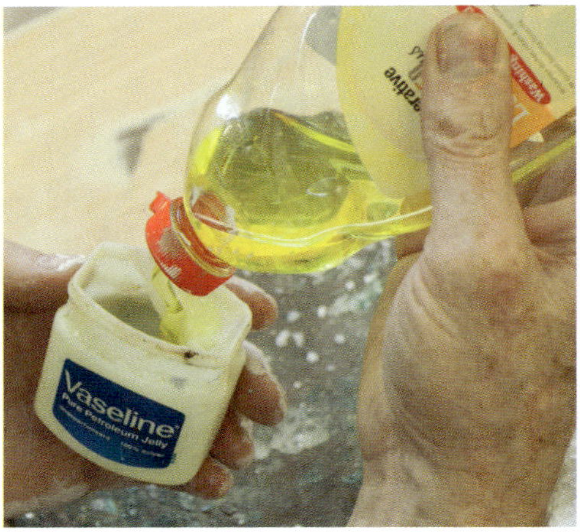

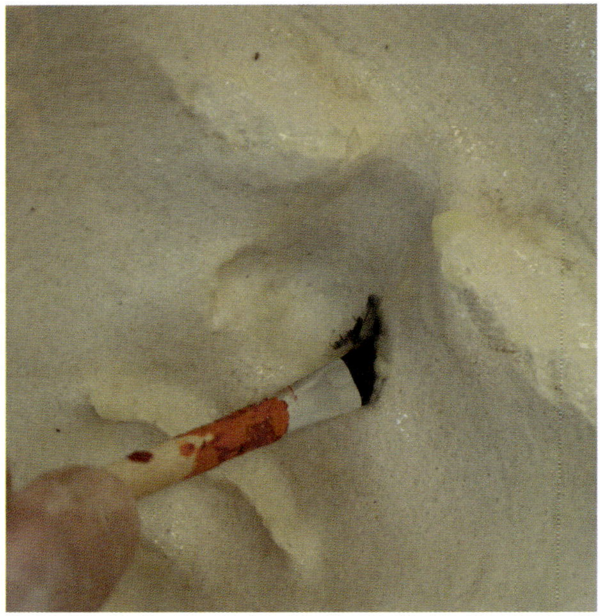

Casting in plaster

Preparing the plaster

Pour 2 inches (5 cm) of tepid water (room temperature) into a standard mixing bowl. Sprinkle plaster lightly into the water. After approximately six bowls'full, a small mountain of plaster should be showing above the surface of the water. That is a sign that the plaster:water ratio is correct.

Stir the bottom of the mixing bowl with a large spoon or your hand until you have a homogeneous plaster solution, like thick cream. Don't mix too vigorously as that will create air bubbles, which will weaken the mould. Keep stirring the plaster until you feel it beginning to thicken. At this point you have about four minutes in which to pour into the mould; this is ample time before the plaster sets, so don't panic!

Pour the plaster gently into the chin of the negative face and tip the plaster around so it leaves an even layer all over. In order to get the plaster up to the edges, tip out the plaster back into the bowl. Repeat this process two or three times, with each 'skin' thickening the layer in the mould.

As the plaster begins to set, it will be necessary to spoon in into the mould in order to start shaping it. Create edges with a 90-degree angle by levelling off the plaster in the mould using a palette knife. With the large spoon dig out a hollow about 2 inches (5 cm) wide along the length of the centre.

Once the plaster has cured and gone hard through the natural process of warming up and cooling down, which can take between 30 to 60 minutes, it is time to remove it from the mould. To release the cast from the plaster bandage mould, place the mould and cast in to a bowl of water, and gradually begin to peal the plaster bandage mould away from the side of the cast, freeing it up. This will be like peeling an orange: it takes some persuasion, yet is easily achieved with only the fingers. The bandage will begin to come apart again, and by peeling it off in the water there is less chance of the face cast cracking.

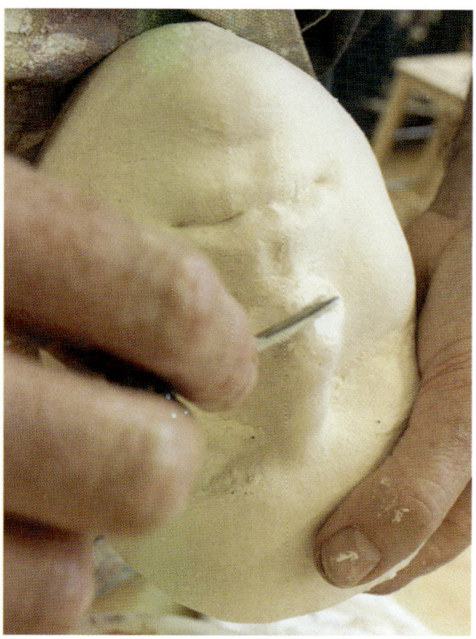

Wash it down with a sponge to remove any of the plaster bandage, Vaseline and washing-up liquid. If there are any lumps of plaster that are not on the original face, trim them off with a modelling tool.

To finish, a coloration from terracotta clay slip will bring it beautifully alive. This is easily achieved by series of simple activities: firstly dilute some dry red terracotta clay in a small amount of water. Mix it with a brush until it is dissolved and thickly paint down the entire case cast until it is evenly covered all over in the brown clay.

Let this stand for a few minutes, and then begin to remove the saturated colour from the high areas of the cast, making highlights with a clean wet sponge. By leaving the saturated colour of the terracotta clay in the contours, the features will be sculpturally enhanced and the relief will look quite life like. As these face casts are of a fleshy colour, and cast from the sitter being upright, they are more life like and resemble a meditating life mask.

Now you will have a base on which to make a mask that fits the owner of the face cast perfectly.

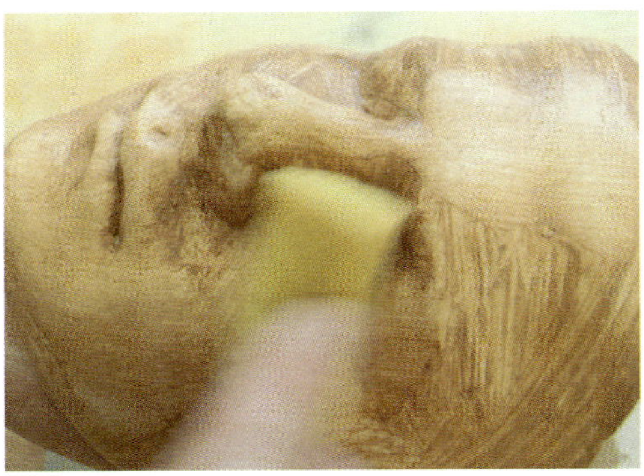

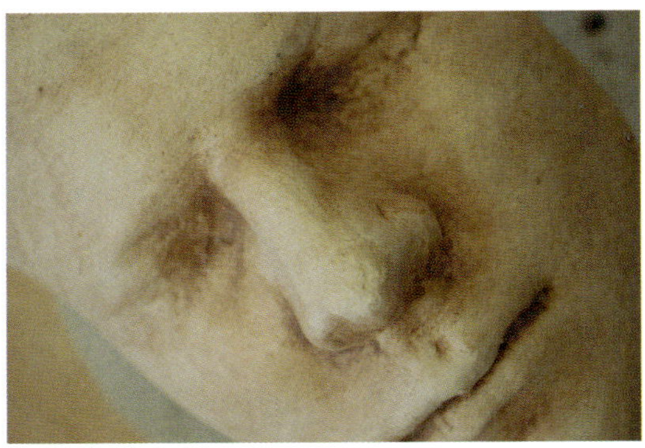

General mask-making techniques

Here are some general mask-making techniques that you can use for the five projects that follow. These techniques are also applicable to the creation of any mask design, large or small, full or half, using simple and effective materials and methods that might possibly have been used hundreds, if not thousands, of years ago. Having created a face cast you will have the base for the next process; if not, there are other ways in which to improvise a solid base form of a face.

Concepts and guidelines for the design of masks in clay

Designing a mask in clay is a personal creative process. The painting of the mask at the end is a continuation of that process, where we are making artistic decisions. In between is the donkey work, which in itself can be fun.

Any effective mask demands careful consideration in terms of design. Obviously you, as the mask maker, can develop a personal style or recognisable traits in your work, although you will also have to interpret the specific requirements of the mask.

The mask could be worn by a performer to enhance a performance; it could be used in education to understand a concept; or in therapy to alleviate pressures of the unknown.

A good mask must allow the user a full range of expression. It should be simple, clean and strong. If the mask is not right, then it will become an obstacle on the face, which will work against both user and observer alike.

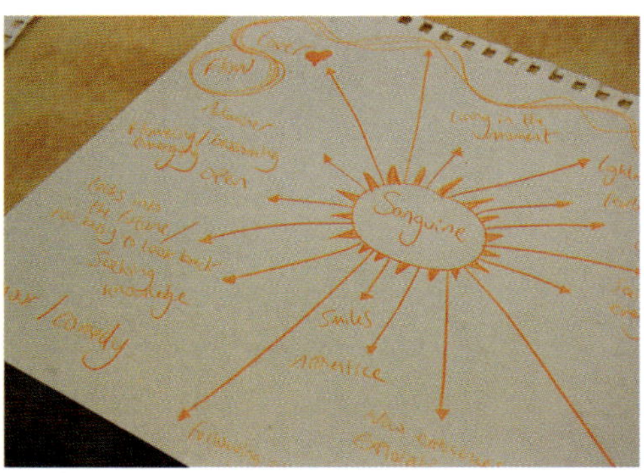

Preparation

Gather as much research material as you can find: text, pictures, ideas from people who will be using the masks, including actors, teachers, therapists, organisational consultants, theatre directors and anyone who might be using the masks you want to make.

Before starting to design a mask ask yourself the following questions:

- How old does the mask need to be?
- What emotions is the mask being required to express?
- What is the mask's status?
- What is its dominant colour?
- What job might the mask have?
- Are they focused in the past present or the future?

Any number of these questions will influence the creation of your mask. In answering them, a picture of the character or archetype will grow in your mind.

The next step is to draw sketches on paper and model small designs in clay, called maquettes; what follows is a general approach to designing a mask though in the next chapter I look specifically at how to design each temperament.

Drawing

It is important to consider the entire physical shape of the body of the person whose mask you're making. At the same time it is not necessary to do a life study; but, as you need to consider the entire body when designing costumes for the stage, you need to think on this scale with a mask. The emphasis is not on the clothes, but rather the body architecture, the expression and energy that flows thought the limbs and the dominant gesture that the mask might suggest.

Body line drawing

The easiest and most fun is to draw without lifting the pencil off the paper, in a continuous way, without stopping to correct. Taking a ball pen or a B3 or B4 graphite pencil and drawing paper, begin to move it round the paper, drawing the arms and legs and head as if the body is in motion. Continuously develop the image gradually until something begins to emerge as a bodily shape that encapsulates the gesture of what the body might be for the mask.

Doodling the head and face

This is a process of scribbling and moving a coloured pencil quickly and spontaneously over the paper to encapsulate the energy and mood of the expression and nature of the character for your mask. Scribble an eye, a mouth, a lip line and a nose. Join them up and find a qualitative gesture, trying to encapsulate the dominant features and expression on the face.

For a half mask, the drawings need to consider how the mask fits onto the whole of the head and face. Drawing curved lines from the ear down the cheeks and joining up on the top lip can make a natural shape. Rather than drawing straight lines that are less organic and natural.

After the drawing, it is time to move into three dimensions.

Maquettes

Maquettes are small working models, usually made in clay without much detail. They are made quickly, by-passing the intellect and working solely in the heel of the hand, the palms and fingers, and finally making some indications for the eyes with a sharp modelling tool at the end.

What is important in this miniature modelling process is to anticipate the general, overall structure of the mask, without worrying about any of the detail, which will come later.

However not everyone works from maquettes; some artists, such as Michelangelo, drew instead in preparation for carving in marble. Henry Moore, on the other hand, made many maquettes as a basis for his sculptures.

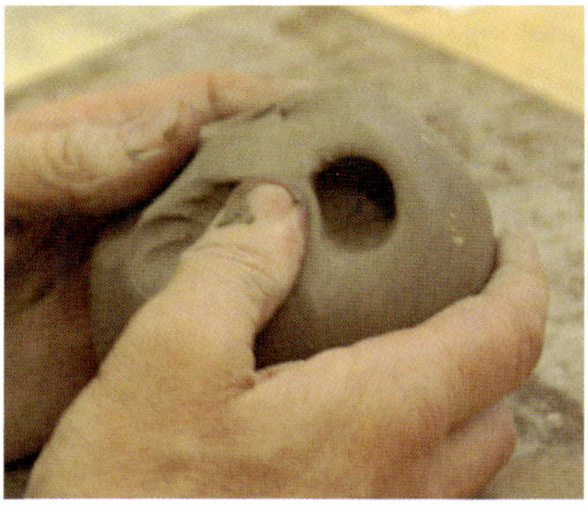

The original clay design

At a certain point in your design preparation you will feel it is time to start in clay. Some people need to sleep on the idea for a night or two before starting the life-size design.

Tools and materials for the clay design

- Clay
- Modelling tools
- Sponge and water
- Vaseline
- Face cast or base, board
- Good light

Modelling base

It can be a great help modelling onto a plaster cast of someone's head, as suggested in the face casting section. If these are not available you can scrunch up some newspaper on a board or model onto a bottle, roughly sculptured polystyrene, or anything that won't hinder your working the clay. Be sure to work onto a firm base.

Design hints

Begin modelling up the design by gathering all your research around you, and preparing your clay in small balls. These can be used to add onto the face cast as you look at the maquette and drawing.

What makes a strong design is the feeling that the mask has both flesh and bones. The bones are solid and unchanging, creating a base upon which the flesh and the muscles of expression can have substance. On this premise, age can be established – for example, does the flesh hang off the bones?

It is very useful to stand back from the design from time to time, looking at it from a distance, moving around to check it from all angles. In so doing, one gets a more objective view of what's going on, where planes and lines are going, or want to go. At this point the mask might start asking for things and the process takes on a two-way conversation. Always remember that masks generally don't 'work' any closer than eight foot.

By observing people around you, their expressions and attitudes, you will notice that the slightest movement of the eyebrow or lip can suggest a change of attitude or expression.

Planes and surfaces

Each feature on the mask has a bearing on all the others. The nose has a relationship to the eyebrow, for example. This can be clarified by smooth, clean planes that run from one to the other. Design is about asking questions, such as where does the brow line end? Does the surface of the cheek run into the lip?

Lines and surfaces meet and join and vanish, and they will demand to go places and meet other areas. If you have an idea, try it but don't get precious about it. Having said this, don't get bogged down by considerations to the detriment of enjoying the clay.

Proportions and dimensions

A mask has to fit and be comfortable. So it is important to consider the dimensions of the mask in relation to the face. Dividers and finger dimensions can be of great assistance. By measuring your own features with your hand, thumb to index finger, and applying that measurement to the clay design, one can, with a little practice, be sure that the mask will fit.

While designing, keep referring to the required size of the mask. Avoid making a helmet mask too small to get on the head; watch out not to make the mask too flat or pancake, as it won't work in profile. Make sure that the design does not stick in or out too much at the edges (for example at the forehead or cheeks) as this will present a problem with the mask fitting.

Symmetry

Try and keep the mask symmetrical, particularly the bone structure. A grossly asymmetrical mask will portray different expressions at different angles. This greatly complicates character portrayal, limiting the actor and confusing the audience.

Modelling tools

Wooden modelling tools can aid the design process immensely, especially when it comes to details around the eye, mouth and nose areas. Bigger modelling tools can help smooth out planes and surfaces. Using the modelling tools is an art in itself, yet the basics are not difficult to manage. Tools are helpful in cleaning up areas that are

rough and uneven, and sometimes too small for your fingers to manage. It is helpful to make sure you have the correct-shaped tool for the modelling you want to clean up.

The metal kidney is helpful for scraping and smoothing large rough surfaces, often around the forehead and cheek areas. The bigger modelling tools are good for defining smaller surfaces and planes like jaws, cheek bones and noses. The finer modelling tools are helpful for getting the details around the eyes, nostrils and mouth. These must only be done last when all the larger planes and surfaces have been finalised.

Finishing off

When you have finished the design, wet a small piece of sponge and gently wipe down the entire mask. This will remove all bumps and indentations, providing a consistent surface. Where the clay meets the modelling base, make sure it does not spread out at the edges. If it does, use a modelling tool to clean it up, as this will create a clean edge to your mould.

Covering

The design is now ready to be cast. If you are not going to cast it immediately, or if you are still working the design and want to leave it for more than a couple of hours, cover it with a wet cloth and a plastic bag so that it does not dry out. If you are going to be covering it in paper for the first layer, put on a release agent to help release the mask from the clay design when it is finished. Vaseline is the best for this purpose.

Mask crafting techniques

Materials and tools for crafting a papier mâché mask

- Vaseline
- Bowls of water
- Polyfilla (interior use)
- PVA glue
- Wallpaper paste
- Inexpensive paint brush
- Sponge
- Plastic modelling tool
- Brown paper
- J-cloth
- Pencil
- Stanley knife
- Scalpel blades (recommended sizes: 10a and 25)
- White spirit
- Cheese wire
- Pair of callipers (optional)
- Towel
- Hairdryer
- Comfortable chair

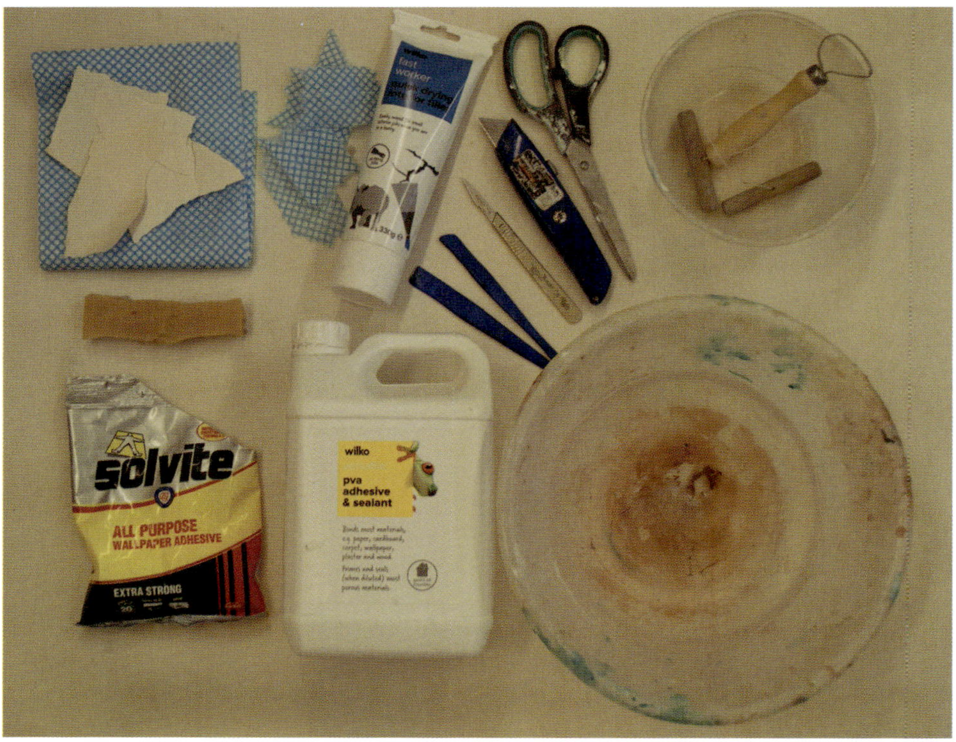

Papier mâché has been used to make such diverse objects as armour, furniture and cutlery, besides puppets and masks. It is strong, hard and cheap, but can take longer than some other mask making materials. Papier mâché is a pleasant way to make masks, as there are no solvents or chemicals to pollute the air.

There are different ways of working with papier mâché. I have had successful results from two methods: one working directly onto the positive design and the other working into a mould (though I don't cover that in this book).

Preparing the surface

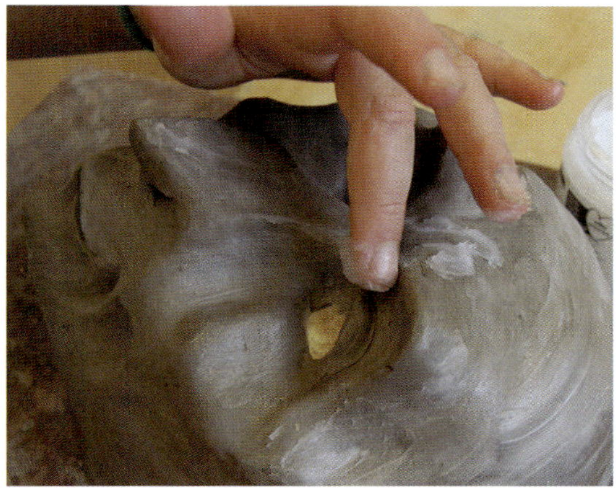

Start by covering the whole design in a thin layer of Vaseline by gently rubbing it on with a finger and a small sponge. Keep it thin and spread evenly all over. This acts as a release agent.

The first layer of brown paper

Use medium-thickness, water-absorbent brown paper. Tear into strips of 2 x 2 inches (5cm) in size. Put the strips of paper into a bowl of warm water and prepare some wallpaper paste.

Cow juice: wallpaper paste and PVA glue

Pour about 1 inch (2.5 cm) of water into a standard-size bowl and slowly sprinkle about four tablespoons of the powdered wallpaper paste into the water while stirring it all the time. After two minutes the water will start to thicken. Add equal part of PVA glue to the wallpaper paste solution and mix slowly. This solution should not be mixed too vigorously, so as to avoid the gelatine getting too runny. Once this mixture is homogenous and thick, like Devon cream, the paste is ready to use.

Method

Dip the brown paper into the solution so it is covered with paste on both sides. Wipe off any excess paste. Prepare a number of pieces of brown paper with the cow juice and let them absorb the mixture while hanging over the side of the bowl. Start at the base and work your way round and up towards the detail on the features of the mask. This will give you time to get to know the process. Apply the pasted paper in small pieces to the (Vaselined) clay design. While applying the paper, make sure there are no air bubbles between the paper and the clay by smoothing them away. When the first piece is secure, supply a second overlapping it on the first by about ½ inch (just over 1 cm). Keep on applying the paper with substantial overlaps until the clay design is completely covered.

When papering over detail and curved areas, use small pieces as this will alleviate any wrinkles. I usually start papering from the base of the clay design (the outside) and work my way up to finish on the nose.

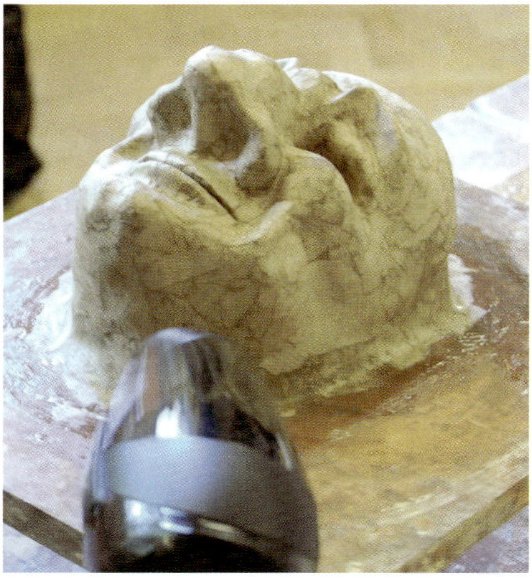

When the first layer has been completed it needs to dry either in the hot sun, or with a hairdryer or by a heater. It should dry sufficiently in about thirty to sixty minutes, at which time you can start the second layer.

The second layer

J-cloths are absorbent cleaning cloths, like a fibrous paper towelling. Tear up the J-cloths into strips, roughly 1 x 2" in size (2.5 x 5 cm).

Sprinkle half a cup of the powdered Polyfilla into a bowl and add some water and mix with the brush. Mix in any lumps of Polyfilla and add any water if the mixture gets too dry and hard. If the mixture is too runny, add some more Polyfilla and thicken it up. Once the mixture has reached a thick but consistent Devon creamy texture, add two tablespoons of PVA glue. Mix this thoroughly until homogenous.

Using the brush, paint a thin layer of Polyfilla onto the first paper layer the size of the piece of J-cloth you are starting with. Place the J-cloth onto the applied Polyfilla and paint over the top of the cloth with more Polyfilla. Repeat this again with the second piece, overlapping as before. Paste the J-cloth onto your first layer of papier mâché, piece by piece as before; however, remember this time to coat the papier mâché with the glue solution before applying the J-cloth. Be aware once again of air bubbles and wrinkles.

To stop any lifting or curling at the edges while drying, extend each layer beyond the bottom of the clay design onto the base board by about ½ an inch (about 1 cm).

The third layer

Dry the second layer with the hairdryer. This layer usually needs less time to dry than the first. When it has dried, apply a third layer, this time returning to the paper. If any bumps, irregularities or air bubbles occur, breaking up a smooth surface and detracting from the original design, they can simply be smoothed out by applying pressure to them with a modelling tool or the back of a paint brush before they are dry.

When you have finished the third layer, give it enough time to thoroughly dry out before removing it from the mould, otherwise pieces of the mask could remain stuck to the inside of the mould. By feeling into the deepest parts one can usually tell when the mask has dried. Use the hairdryer to dry out the entire mask before cutting and removing the clay from the inside. When the mask has dried, proceed with the cutting.

Cutting and removing the mask from the clay design

When trimming and cutting the excess edge off the mask, consider three things: aesthetics, symmetry and fitting. Firstly, the edge of the mask has a bearing on the whole, and has a relationship to the rest of the mask.

Symmetry is important so that the mask does not look too different form each side, which would create a different character. Asymmetry can be interesting in some masks; however the danger is that the mask might look disfigured and present big challenges in using it.

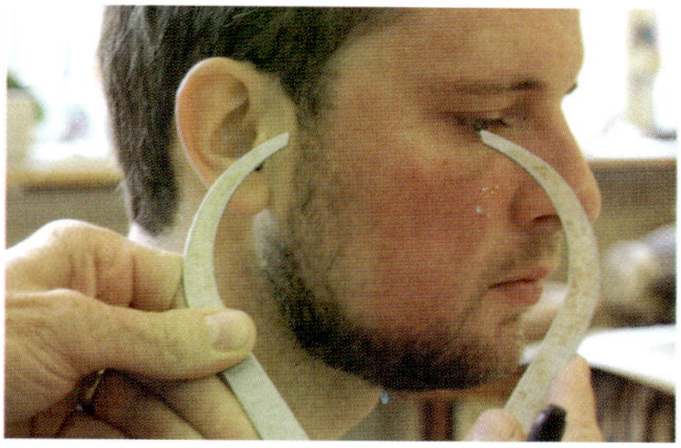

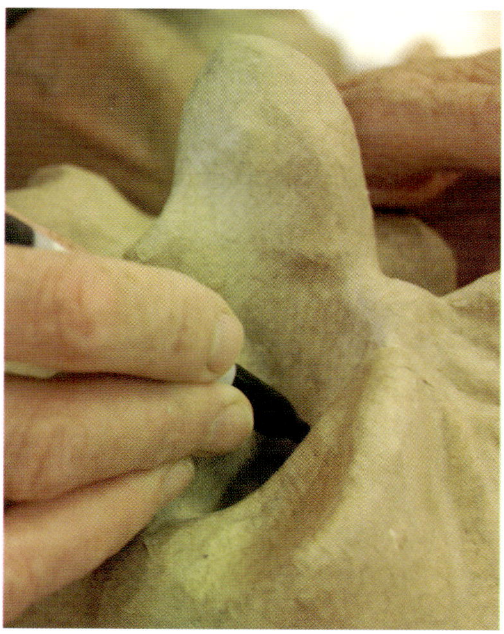

The third consideration is cutting the mask to fit and be comfortable. The best way to do this is to trying the mask on and cut to the following rule of thumb: hair line to just under the chin; ear to ear. Using a pair of callipers to measure the distance from the ear to the eye can assist in cutting the mask to fit.

Cutting

To keep the mask symmetrical, draw the lines you want to cut, first on one side and then exactly the same on the other side. Draw the eye and the nostril cut lines too. The eyes do not want to be too deep. The rule of thumb is ¼ inch (4 mm) for an eyelid or nostril is as deep as you want to go. In going deeper the danger is that the eyes will stick into the eyes of the wearer.

Having drawn the line of the outer edge, use the Stanley knife to cut along the line. You have done the design work in preparing the cut, now consider the technical use of the knife. Push the knife into the mask, through the three layers and into the clay behind. This will back up the cut, making it smooth and clean. The mask is still fragile and flexible, as it will take a number of days to dry out thoroughly, so the clay support

is helpful in keeping the shape of the mask. Having pushed the Stanley knife into the cut line, slowly pull the knife along the line. Keep the blade at a 90⁰ angle to the mask, and cut in one continuous line. Having cut all the way round, remove the outer flange. Proceed now to cut out the eyes and nostrils with the scalpel blades, using the 10a for the nostrils and the 25 for the eyes. Once again cut in a smooth continuous line, as the better the line cut into the clay, the easier the transition to finishing off the outer edges. The outer edge can be peeled off to assist in releasing the mask from the mould.

Releasing the mask from the mould

With the outer edges removed, release the entire design from the board with a cheese wire. Sit comfortably in a low chair, put a towel in your lap, and place the mask and clay design face down in your lap between your legs.

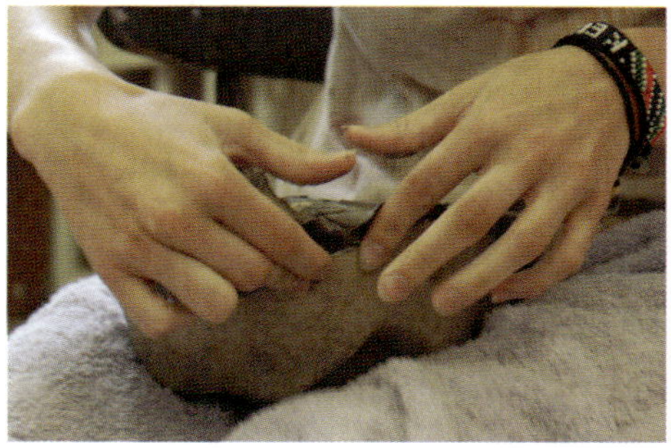

With a wire modelling tool, remove as much of the clay from the design as possible, and release the plaster face cast from the design. Dig out as much of the clay as you can from the sides, and see if you can fold the sides in and take the rest of the clay out in one go. Ease it out of the mould bit by bit, working it loose all the way round, until it pops out.

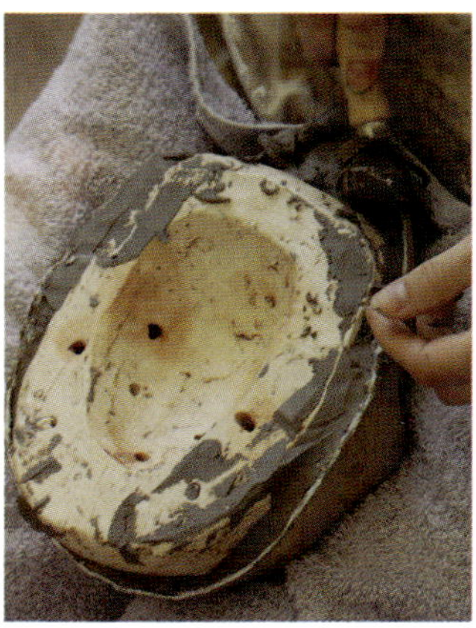

Going outdoors for ventilation, wipe the Vaseline off the inside of the mask with a cloth dipped in white spirit.

This is a good moment to clear up all the clay and paper, the plaster cast and board, and prepare for the next task. Using the hairdryer, dry off the white spirit and give the mask time to harden, anything from fifteen minutes to half an hour depending on the size of the masks, before the next process.

Finishing the edges

Once the mask has been cut out it will be necessary to finish the edges. Cover any exposed edges with a thin layer of papier mâché in the manner of the first and third layers. This time fold the small pieces of papier mâché from the inside over the edge to the outside, smoothing it out so there are no wrinkles. Repeat this with a second and third layer, overlapping all the while as you go along. When the entire outer edges have been covered, including the eyes and nostrils with small pieces of paper, take the opportunity to cover any areas that you might have missed with the third layer of paper. Using the hairdryer for the last time, dry the mask thoroughly. This usually takes anything from fifteen minutes to half an hour.

Painting and colouring

Some masks need very little or no colour at all, in which case paint a strong protective varnish onto the brown paper finish, which will protect the surface and give it a slight shine to reflect in the lights. Most masks benefit from coloration of some kind or another. I will give you the basic strong and effective painting technique (though there are others that are effective for different materials, styles and functions). This technique is very useful on top of brown paper masks, giving them a rich hue and vibrancy, bringing life to the features you have created in the design.

Colouring the mask is the next creative process after the design. This again is a personal preference, but the colour has a strong bearing on the requirements of the mask. Character, style and overall design for the function have to be considered.

Masks can be coloured with almost anything from acrylic paints, oil paint, poster paint, gouache and enamel to boot polish, ink and vegetable dyes. These all have vastly different effects. The most versatile is acrylic paint, which is water based, not too expensive and quick to dry. I have outlined below three methods of colouring with acrylic paint. They have different effects and can be used in conjunction with one another.

As with the designing, painting is a very personal and artistic process. Choosing the colours, the tones and hues will be considered in more detail as we look at the four main projects of each of the temperament masks. Here is the basic technique in a nutshell.

Materials and tools

- Brushes
  Round ¼-inch (6 mm) brush with long bristles for wet painting.
  Round 1-inch (2.5 cm) brush for dry brushing.
  Round ½-inch (1 cm) brush with short bristles for highlights.
- Paint
  A raft of tones of acrylic paint from a deep dark colour, a mid-range of the same hue over the base coat, and a highlight of a lighter tone but similar hue.
- Jar of water
- Brown paper for testing
- Apron

Paint swabs

Paint each of the colours onto a piece of brown paper to see how they fit together next to each other. You might need to adjust one of the tones by adding more or less colour

to get the contrasts at a good level. If the contrasts are too extreme, or not extreme enough, the effect can lack contrast and expressiveness. You will need to experiment until you get a good combination of tones.

The base coat

This is the darkest tone being used in colouring your mask. It is painted on wet over the brown paper of the mask, so beware not to make the paint too runny, as this could make the outside layer lift off or distort a little. Using the small, long-bristled brush, paint this on all over the entire outside of the mask. Keep the colour just up to the outer edge in a clean line. The base coat needs to be consistent all over, taking care to fill in all the brown of the mask. This can take two coats, again making sure it's not too runny.

The second coat

This is the mid range, which is done in a different technique called dry-brushing. Dry-brushing is one of the most popular painting techniques for the theatrical mask as it is simple, effective and quick. Because of extreme colour contrasts, dry brushing will allow the mask to project over a great distance while close up this technique can look overbearing.

Dry-brushing uses the paint as thick as it comes – directly from the tube. Using brush two, the harder-bristled brush, dip it into the paint, and then make sure it is evenly spread all over the base of the brush by firmly brushing it off onto the brown paper; then lightly brush onto the high points of the mask.

The lighter colour will deposit itself onto the dark paint in a sunburst effect bringing out a strong highlight. By using lighter and lighter colours, build up a strong, but gradual, contrast. A tip with this technique is to apply the colour minimally to start with, gradually extending it over the mask while still leaving as much of the dark base exposed as possible.

The highlights

The final coat of colour, the highlight, is done with the smallest brush and is the same technique as dry-brushing. Now painting with the lightest tones only cover the highest points of the mask and the ridges, usually including the forehead, cheekbones, chin, eyelids, nose and lips. Get an even, symmetrical distribution of colour over the mask. If the colour gets saturated and becomes too dense in one spot, stipple some mid-range or base coat over the offending place and start with the highlight from the top. Once you are happy with the results (and this might mean taking a break and returning to it later to be objective enough to see it for what it is), you will need to seal the mask.

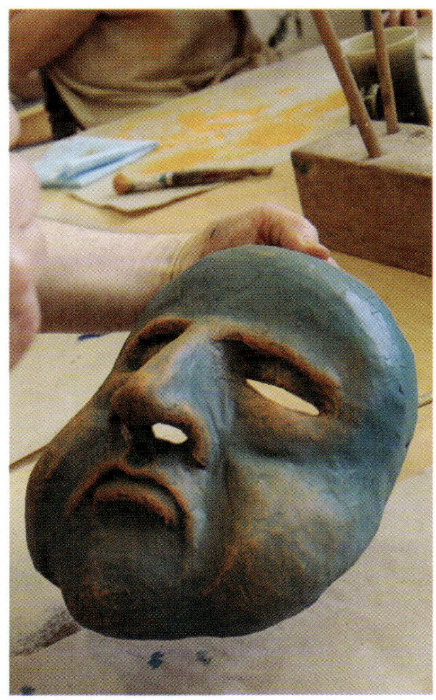

Finishing

Finally to finish off the mask you will need to varnish it, put elastic in it to fit it to the head and foam it for comfort.

Tools and materials

- Acrylic spray varnish: small can of eggshell or matt finish
- Respiration mask
- Hole-punch used for leather
- Pencil
- Elastic ½ inch (1 cm) wide (black)
- Contact adhesive glue: applied to both surfaces and left to dry for a minute before sticking to each other
- Pieces of soft foam: 4 pieces of 2 x 1 x ½" (5 x 2.5 x 1cm)

Varnishing

When the mask has been painted, it is important to fix the colour. This will give it a slight shine. A completely matt mask will soak up light, lose definition and look flat. Various varnishes can be used from clear spray lacquer to boat varnish.

Polyurethane varnishes, like boat varnish, can offer good protection to the mask surface. Shellac is a varnish that is very quick drying and is not too shiny, but it is slightly pigmented and can detract from the original colouring. Avoid high gloss varnishes as they create reflection problems and become quite garish. When spraying on the varnish, take care to keep the spray can at least 8 inches (20 cm) from the mask, and spray it in painting gestures first around the base, then gradually move up and around the mask covering it evenly as you go. Place the mask in front of a heater or use a hair-dryer to dry the varnish and get rid of the smell.

Holes and elastic

Once the varnish has dried, make holes in the mask for the elastic. A good leather punch makes the most clean and exact holes. By putting the mask on and feeling the edge in relation to your ears, you can ascertain the best place to attach the elastic. In attaching the elastic too high, or too low, the mask might hang forward, or not sit correctly on the face so take care and experiment before making the holes. The rule of thumb is to take a pencil and, measuring a line from the eye to the ear, where the arm of a pair of glasses might go, make a mark about a quarter of an inch (6 mm) from the edge of the mask. Punch the holes on the middle of the mark by squeezing the hole punch with both hands. Usually you can hear a click as the punch cuts through the layers of the mask. Use a ½-inch (1 cm) wide black elastic and attach it through the holes in the mask with a double knot.

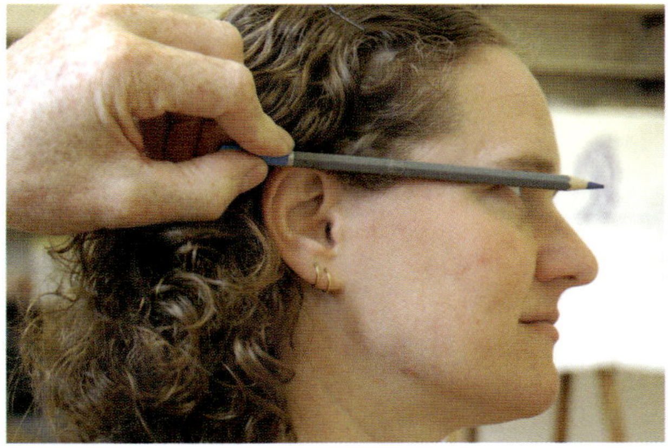

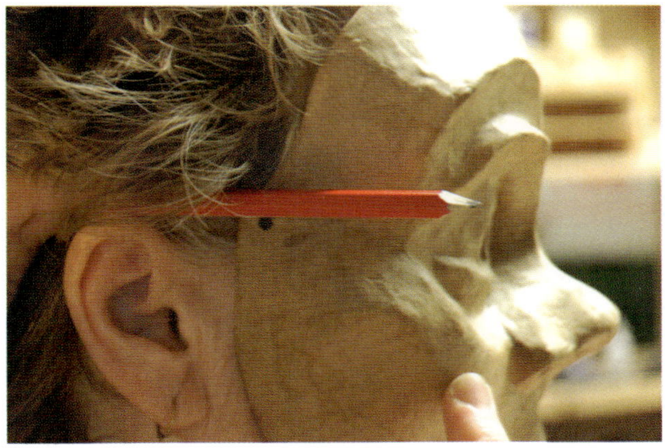

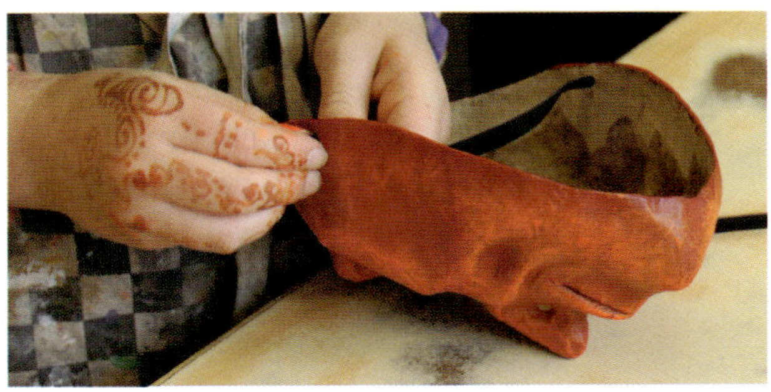

With a half mask, when putting it on to mark the place for the elastic holes, make sure the top lip of the mask is over the top lip of the person wearing it. Then mark for the whole.

Fitting the mask

If the mask does not fit exactly or is slightly uncomfortable, glue small pieces of soft foam onto the inside of the mask. The places where this is most helpful are on the forehead, the cheeks, the bridge of the nose and/or the cheekbone area. The foam pieces need be no bigger than 1 x 1 x ½ " (2.5 x 2.5 x 1.2 cm) and no more than three in total will be necessary. Apply the contact adhesive to both the foam and the mask surfaces, allowing them one minute to dry and then placing the foam onto the designated area.

Trying the mask on

It is always good to take time to try the mask on and see how it works. For more ideas, look at Chapter 4, where I explore ideas about the life of the mask. If you have been working in a group it is great to take a 'family portrait' with participants in their masks, and another with them in each other's masks.

Chapter 3

MAKING MASKS OF THE TEMPERAMENTS

Having introduced the general mask-making techniques from design to construction and finishing, I would like to hone in on specific considerations for making masks of each of the four temperaments and the neutral. I will only consider the areas specific to each temperament, and refer the reader to the general chapter for specifics on techniques applicable to all masks (Chapter 2). These are suggestions and considerations for an approach that I trust you will make your own.

Tools and materials for the clay design

- Ball pen or a B3 or B4 graphite pencil
- Drawing paper
- Clay
- Modelling tools
- Sponge and water
- Vaseline
- Face cast or base
- Board

Having created a face cast you will have the base for the next process; if not, a base for modelling on can be created on a bottle, some wet, scrunched-up newspaper just smaller than a face size on a board or the plaster cast from some plastic mask that you might find in a joke shop.

Materials and tools for painting

- Brushes

  Round ¼-inch (6 mm) brush with long bristles for wet painting.

  Round 1-inch brush for dry brushing.

  Round ½-inch (1 cm) brush with short bristles for highlights.
- Paint (references to specific colour for each temperament will accompany each project)
- Jar of water
- Brown paper for testing

In painting a full or half mask, the same materials tools and methods apply.

Designing and painting a melancholic mask

Getting a feel for the mask

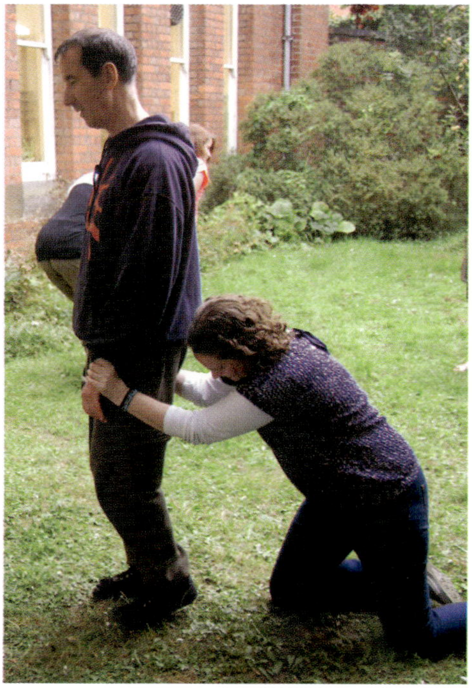

The melancholic temperament is experienced predominantly in the bones, connected to the element of earth. To enter into the design it can be very helpful to look at a hard stone or feel some bone of an animal, for example, and see how it forms the structural basis upon which the rest of the body is situated.

Write a list of all the words that come to mind on the theme of earth. This is not moist soil, which has water in it, nor is it light dust, or volcanic lava. Words such as 'hard', 'bony', 'rock', 'blue', 'deep', 'stone', 'pain', 'skeleton' and 'death' can come up. With these words in mind, try to around the room as if you are filled with stones, feel the slow dragging gestures as if gravity has become more of a resistance than before.

Use the interactive body-work exercises from Chapter 6 (p 126), which includes the 'dragging' exercise. Find a fellow mask maker to sit on the floor behind you and hold onto them as if you were holding two heavy shopping bags. Walk slowly, dragging them along behind you. Take care not to fight the resistance by using your muscles, but instead resign to the act of carrying, using your skeleton. Observe what this activity does to your facial muscles, which facial muscle set becomes dominant? Keeping the expression on your face, ask a friend to mirror back what they see your face doing. Briefly and spontaneously draw what you see going on in their face. Look in a mirror and see what is going on in your face as you do this dragging motion. This might look like you normally do; if so, it could well be that you have an element of the melancholic temperament. Whatever the case, use the image of this feeling as a guide for your drawing, which follows.

Drawing the Melancholic

The three stages of drawing, from the continuous line for the body, the doodle for the face and the life-size drawing, front on and profile, are useful to have as a reference when leading up to the final design in clay.

Body line drawing

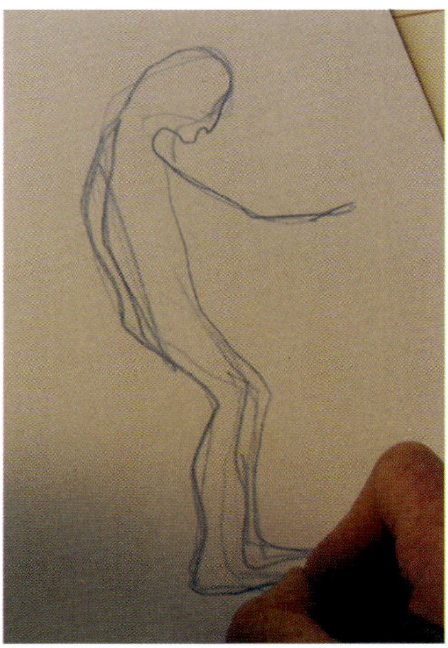

As with the design suggestions in the previous chapter, this activity is spontaneous and playful, but is more focused on the temperament. Having moved as the temperament, draw it with a continuous line without lifting the pen off the paper, drawing the arms, legs and head as if the body is in motion. Continue to develop the image until something begins to emerge as a bodily shape that encapsulates the gestures of the Melancholic. The question I always ask myself is: am I genuinely trying to capture the melancholic bodily form, or am I just going into something that looks and feels good? What looks and feels good will not necessarily encapsulate the temperament.

Doodling the head and face

This is a process of scribbling and moving a coloured pencil quickly and spontaneously over the paper to encapsulate the energy and mood of the facial expression and nature of the temperament. Scribble an eye, a mouth, a lip line and a nose. Join them up and find a qualitative gesture that feels appropriate for the Melancholic. Blues are helpful for the melancholic mood, even if the temperament is not a mood as such, but rather a constitutional and more fixed aspect of the human countenance.

Front-on and profile drawing

The emphasis is on the life-size nature of the drawing. Start by drawing two egg-shaped spheres, one upright and the other on an angle, about the size of a human head. In a balanced drawing of a face, from the hairline to the bottom of the chin the proportions will be equal between the thinking, feeling and willing part of the head. For the Melancholic, the feeling third, the middle sphere, will need to be emphasised, both in the front-on drawing and in profile. Here are two examples: play around and make them your own.

Making a maquette

Without worrying about the detail, but keeping in mind a sense of the form to come, begin with a round ball. And, as with the drawing, begin to lengthen the sphere. What the mask maker needs to do is to emphasise the bones in the face, to bring out the boniness of the Melancholic. The boniness does not necessarily mean age, as long as the flesh does not hang off it. The bones are the hard places in the design, the forehead, the cheekbones, chin and nose bridge. This skull-like quality, emphasising the length of the face, is a good indication of the melancholic temperament.

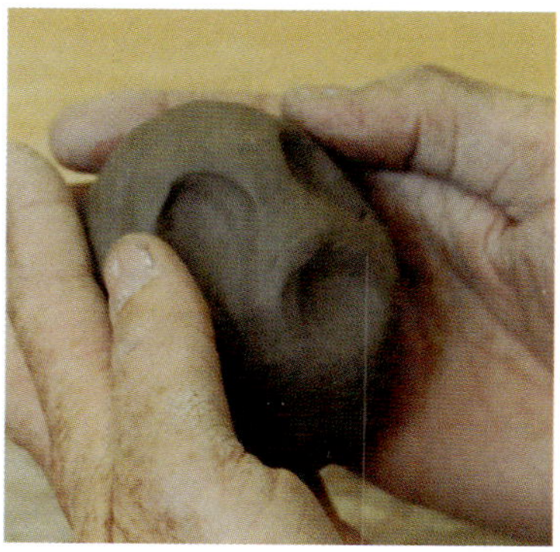

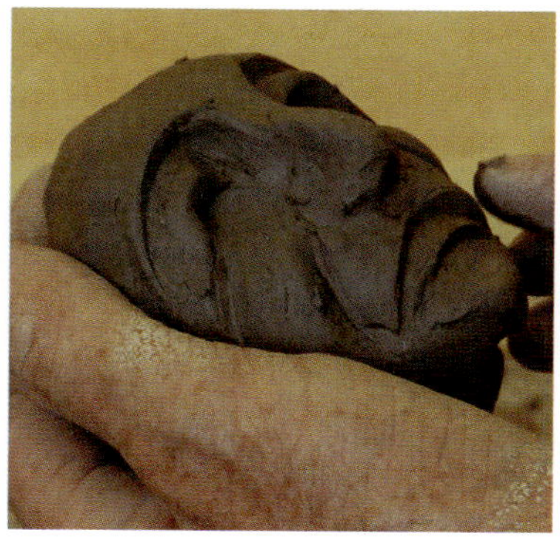

The full design

The process of making a mask can take a while. It is best done over a number of sessions, with perhaps even a night in between. This will give you time to see your work afresh and can give new insights about what needs to be developed in your design as you go along.

Having gathered the reference materials around you, along with a face cast (see Chapter 2) on a board with the small modelling balls of clay at the ready, start by accentuating the skull.

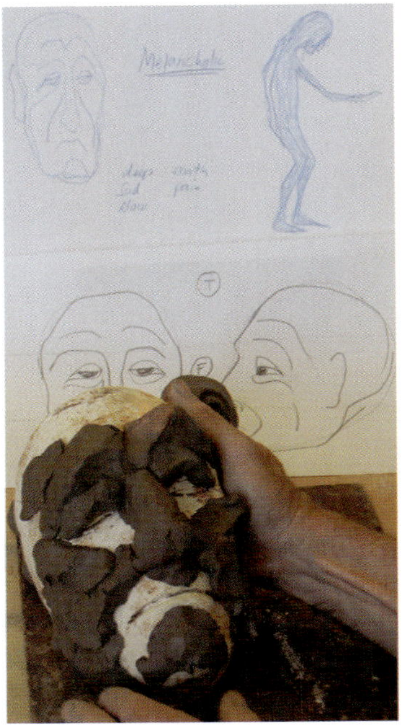

Continue with the nose, jaw and chin. and finish with flesh around the lips and eyelids.

For designing a half melancholic mask, the following considerations can be helpful: take the top lip of the mask into the top lip of the face cast. From the side of the lips on either side take the clay down onto the cheek a little, and then let it sweep up toward the ears. For the melancholic specifically, use the clay to make a full lip, drooping down from the centre of the top lip, and also down from the corners of the mouth.

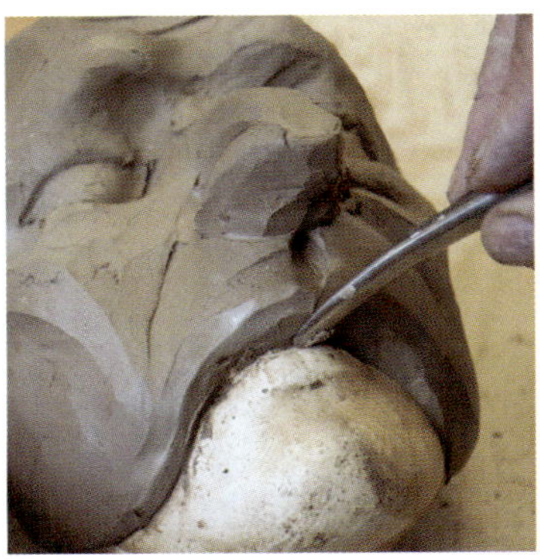

Having designed the mask, wash it, Vaseline it and cover it with the three layers as demonstrated in Chapter 2 (pp 34–38). When the mask has been completed with the outer layer being papered and dried, you can move onto the painting of the melancholic mask.

Painting the Melancholic

Paint colours for the Melancholic might include: a raft of blue tones of acrylic paint from a deep dark blue, a mid-range of the same hue of blue to go over the base coat, and a highlight of a lighter tone of blue but similar hue.

Please see Chapter 2 for materials and processes you use to paint the mask, including how to use tones from dark to light to enhance the dramatic nature of the mask. For this mask we are focusing on the blue tones and hues characteristic of the Melancholic. Get a piece of brown paper from which you made the mask, and look at the colours and how they work together. Put a brush stroke of the base coat, the mid range and the highlight next to each other to see how they look together before painting the mask.

The base coat

With the darkest tone you have the opportunity to go into the deep French blues, perhaps with a little red to bring warmth to it. Paint this on all over the entire outside of the brown paper mask. Keep the colour just up to the outer edge, not too wet, and give it two layers to cover the surface entirely.

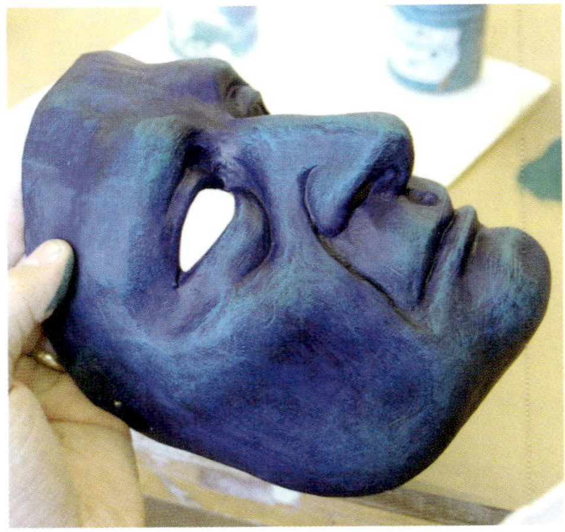

The second coat

With the mid-range tone, use dry-brushing: start by wiping off any excess paint from the brush, then lightly brush in a dusting motion onto the high points of the mask. Build up a strong, but gradual contrast, applying the colour minimally to start with, gradually extending it over the mask, while still leaving as much of the dark base exposed.

The highlights

Painting with the lightest tones, only cover the highest points of the mask, including (usually) the forehead, the eyelids, the nose and lips. Get an even, symmetrical distribution of colour over the mask.

Having painted the three layers of colour over the mask, take the opportunity to varnish it with the acrylic spray varnish, and punch the holes also as described in Chapter 2. The mask is now ready for fitting and wearing.

Designing and painting a phlegmatic mask

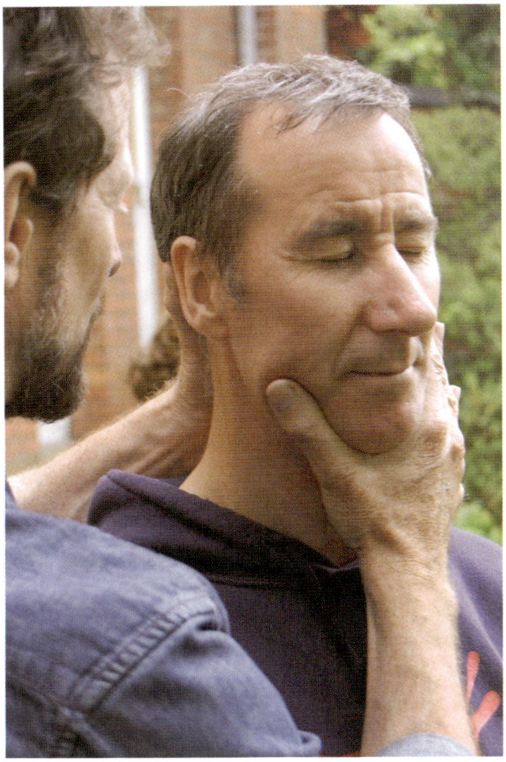

Getting a feel for the mask

Human beings are made up of over 70 per cent water, which passes through the lymph glands as it moves around the body making up the immune system. In creating a mask that has the qualities of the phlegmatic temperament, in can be helpful to observe the element of water. Look at water in a glass; it does not have a shape of its own, but takes the form of the container. When water freezes it goes hard like stone; when it boils, it creates steam. Water in its most natural state is still; only in regard to the other elements does it taken on the power of the sea or a river, or the rain in a storm.

Write a list of all the words that come to mind on the theme of water: maybe 'wet', 'life-giving', 'shapeless' might occur. With these words in mind, try to move in the quality of water, exploring slow, calm, floating movements and gestures.

Use the interactive body-work exercises in Chapter 6 (pp 111–114), which include 'floating': find a fellow mask maker to take the weight of your head and relieve you of the responsibility of carrying it around. By holding your partner's head with one of your hands at the back of their head, the other just under the chin, not constricting the breathing, slightly lift their head and invite them to let you take their weight. Once you feel they have given you the weight of their head, still holding it, invite them to take a step forward, then another until they are walking round the room supported by your hands taking the weight of their head. After a few steps, let them go into free walking, but to keep the feeling of being supported, and not making waves, but keeping calm and tranquil. Swap this over to have the experience yourself.

Keep this experience as a reference of a 'water person', which is a key for getting in touch with the Phlegmatic. Using this experience, proceed with the drawing.

Drawing the Phlegmatic

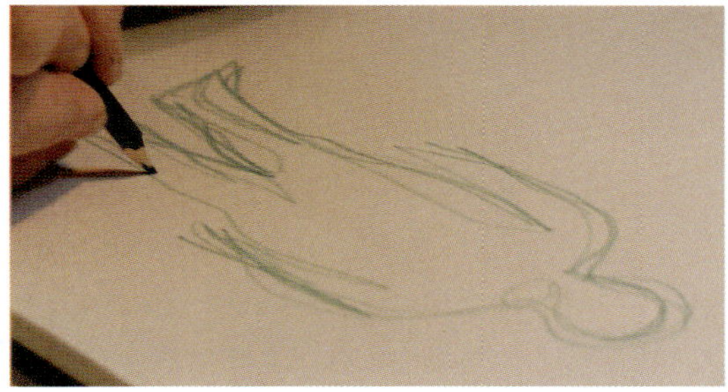

The sketches you make here will be used as references when you come to make the final mask.

Body line drawing

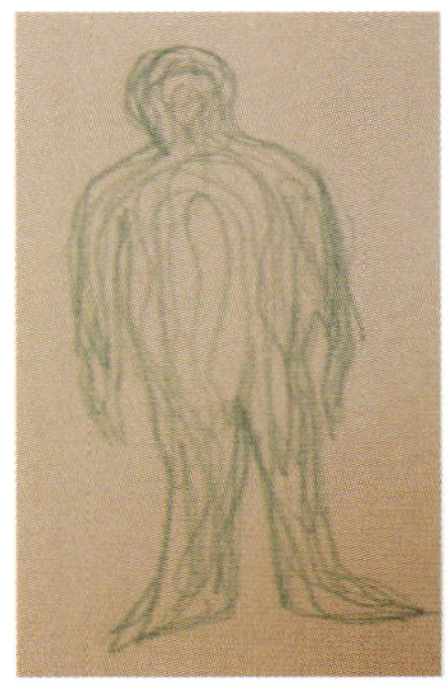

Having moved as the temperament, take a coloured pencil and drawing paper, and draw a continuous line round the paper, describing the arms, legs and head as if the body is in calm motion. Develop the image gradually with as many lines as you need until something begins to emerge as a bodily shape encapsulating phlegmatic movement, shape and gesture.

Doodling the head and face

Encapsulate the mood of the expression and nature of the phlegmatic temperament by energetic scribbling. See the 'Doodling' section for the melancholic temperament (p 27) for more detail. Greens are very useful in producing a calm and balanced mood for the Phlegmatic.

Front on and profile

Draw two eggshaped spheres, one upright and the other on an angle, about the size of a human head. For the Phlegmatic there is a general roundness about the head and face, without any features being too striking. The thinking and feeling sphere tends to be more exaggerated with less emphasis on the willing, where the chin and neck can become rounded.

Making a maquette

Taking a ball of clay big enough to fit between the palms of your hands, round it off to a smooth sphere. Without thinking about the detail, begin to form some features in the middle of the sphere, indicating the eyes, nose and mouth. What you need to emphasise with the Phlegmatic is roundness and soft, flowing form. The wateriness is in the formless soft places of the cheeks, the eyelids and the lips, accentuating the fleshiness without bringing in muscle, bone or the pointedness of the other temperaments.

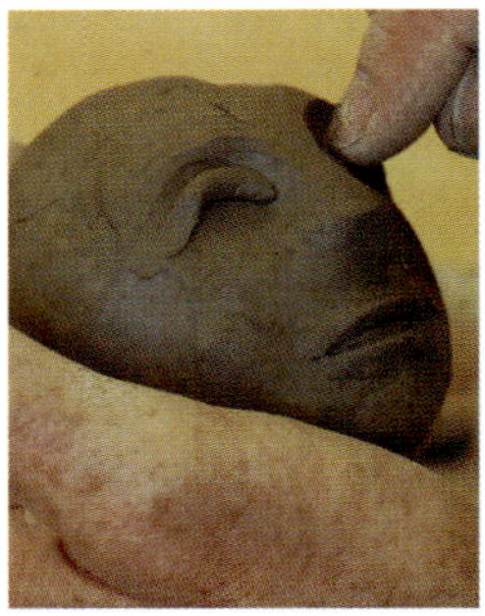

The full design

Gather the reference material around you – drawings, the maquette, pictures and words, along with a face cast on a board (see Chapter 2). Begin by applying the small modelling balls of clay, accentuating the roundness of the face.

Continue by developing the features in a soft and inexpressive way and finish with soft flowing features.

For designing a half phlegmatic mask, the following can be helpful: take the top lip of the mask into the top lip of the face cast. Keep the lip line straight, sculpting it neither up nor down, but rather using the clay make a full but soft lip without any undue muscle tension lip,

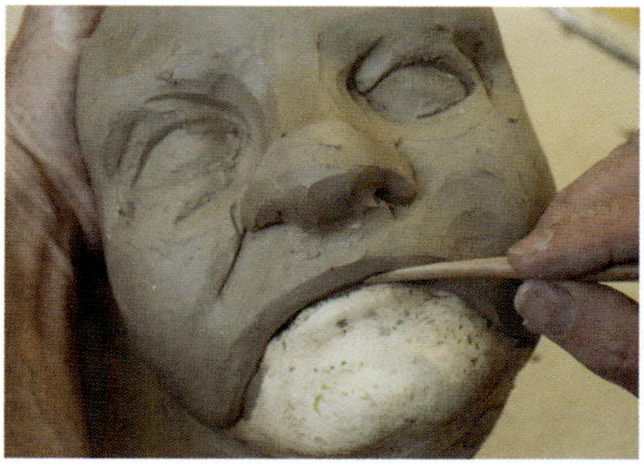

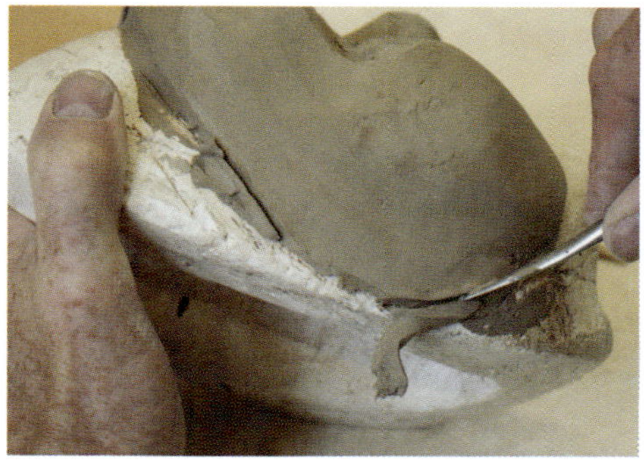

with a straight line from the centre of the top lip to the corners of the mouth. From the side of the lips on either side take the clay down onto the cheek a little, and then let it sweep up toward the ears.

Having designed the mask, go through all the steps of creating the mask out of the layers of paper and cloth, cutting, releasing, finishing the outer edge and drying it off, before continuing with painting (see Chapter 2, pp 42–45, for instructions).

Painting the Phlegmatic

Using the guidance on painting from the Chapter 2, focus now on the green tones and hues. Create your swab on brown paper from which you made the mask and look at the colours and how they work together, finding the greens for the base coat, the mid range and the highlights.

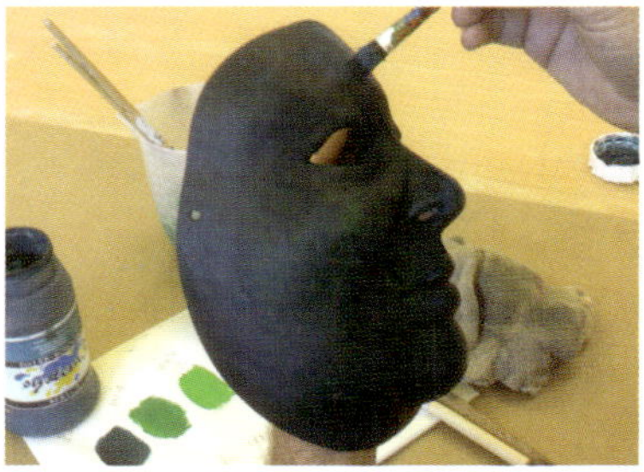

The base coat

Being the darkest of the tones, the deep green will offer a good base for the lighter tones to come (though take care not to go too dark). Paint this on all over the entire outside of the brown paper mask, keeping the colour just up to the outer edge, not too wet, and give it two layers to cover the surface entirely.

The second coat

Dry brush using the mid-range colour (see p 45 for details), applying your chosen mix of mid-green. Remember to start by wiping off any excess paint from the brush, then lightly brush onto the high points of the mask. Build up a strong but gradual contrast of mid green over the base coat, extending it over the mask while still leaving as much of the dark base exposed as possible.

The highlights

With the lightest and brightest tones of blue, perhaps with a degree of lemon yellow in them, cover the highest points of the mask, including the forehead, the eyelids, nose and lips. Get an even symmetrical distribution of colour over the mask.

Having coloured the mask, varnish it and punch the holes as described in Chapter 2 (pp 46–47). The mask is now ready for fitting and wearing.

Designing and painting a sanguine mask

Getting a feel for the mask

Look at a leaf blowing in the wind, how unpredictable its journey is as it makes its way to the ground. It might suddenly take off again and be difficult to catch. This is a good image to have in mind when considering the Sanguine, which is based on the nervous system, continuously responding to external stimuli.

The nervous system passes information from the periphery of the body to the brain very quickly. This rapid activity of the nervous system has often been associated with the element of air. Descriptions that come to mind on the theme of air are often: 'light', 'moveable', 'changeable', 'unpredictable', 'playful', 'yellow', 'in the present'. This is not the howling winds created by high pressure but the light movement of air responding to the everyday changes of temperature. With these words in mind, move in the quality of air, find the light, playful, unpredictable and unexpected gestures.

Using simple interactive body work of responding to external stimuli, find a fellow mask maker and explore the following exercise: one of you (A) stand in a calm neutral position, while the other (B) gives indications for movement by lightly pushing the hand of A, allow the impulse of movement to carry on as if being blown by the wind. Repeat this with another part of the body, the shoulder, for example. B originates the movement, and A responds, continuing it in the direction of the impetus. B needs to allow the impetus to finish before giving the next indication to move. In this way A will be moved around like a leaf in the wind.

Using this experience of being externally stimulated, take up the paper and pencil and capture the experience on paper.

Drawing the Sanguine

It's really good to get a feel for these drawings, as you will use them to inform the final design.

Body line drawing

Having moved as the sanguine temperament, draw it with a continuous line without

lifting the pencil off the paper. Taking some drawing paper and a yellow colouring pencil and begin drawing the arms, legs and head, developing the image gradually over and over until something begins to emerge as a bodily shape that encapsulates the gesture of Sanguine.

Doodling the head and face

Scribble quickly and spontaneously over the paper to encapsulate the energy, mood and facial expressions of the sanguine temperament. Oranges and yellows are helpful for this temperament mood, giving vibrancy and energy to the drawing.

Front on and profile

Draw two egg shapes, one upright and the other tilted on an angle, about the size of a human head, emphasising the feeling middle realm of the face. Begin to explore this temperament in three dimensions in the clay.

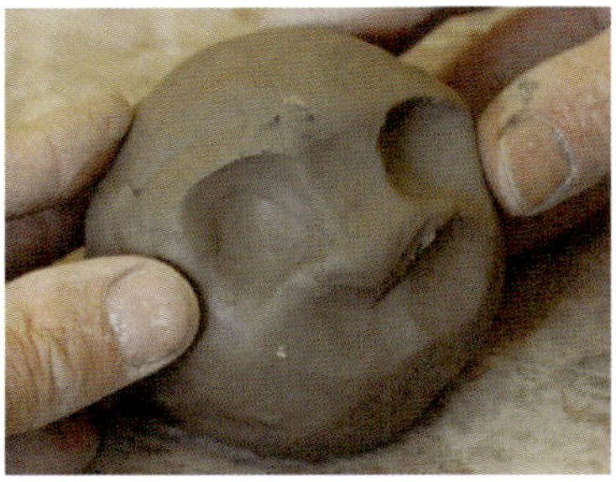

Making a maquette

What the Sanguine needs to express is an alertness, an awareness of the senses expressed in the eyes, the nostrils and the lips. This does not necessarily mean making the mask look young: even old sanguine people have a child's light in their faces. The nerves bring an aliveness to the features, without emphasising the bones or muscles.

The full design

With a face cast on a board (see Chapter 2, p 28–33) and the reference material around you, begin to apply the small modelling balls of clay to the cast, start with the middle of the face and the features – the eyes, nose and lips. Try to create an expression of keen interest by emphasizing the open eyes and uplifted mouth. Finish with the typical attribute of the sanguine, the smile.

 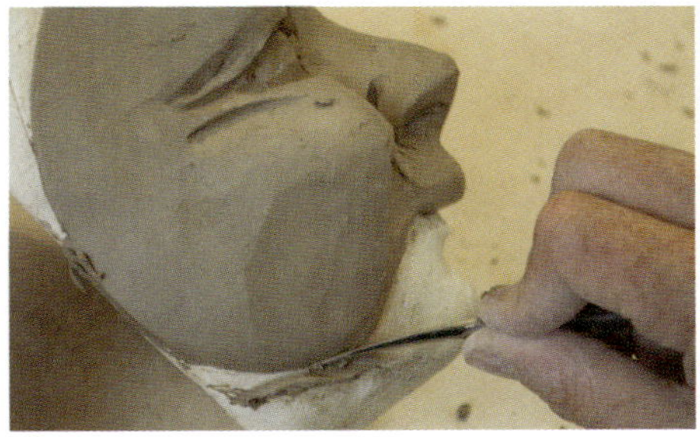

For designing a half sanguine mask, this might be helpful: take the top lip of the mask into the top lip of the face cast. Keep the lip line curving upward slightly from the centre, using the clay to make muscle tension in the lip with a smile from the centre of the top lip to the corners of the mouth. From the side of the lips on either side take the clay down onto the cheek a little, and then let it sweep up toward the ears.

Follow the instructions in Chapter 2 (pp 34–42) for how to apply the three layers of paper and material and how to cut and dry it before moving onto the painting of the sanguine mask.

Painting the Sanguine

Create a swab of the three colour tones and hues. Working with a deep yellow and beige as a base tone, an orangey yellow as a mid range and a lemon yellow and white as a highlight, place them next to each other on the brown paper, and see if they work in combination. If they don't, it can be helpful to put some of the base-coat brown into the mid-range orange and some of the mid-range orange into the lemon yellow highlight. It might be that they need to be brought into a closer relation to each other in order to jar less.

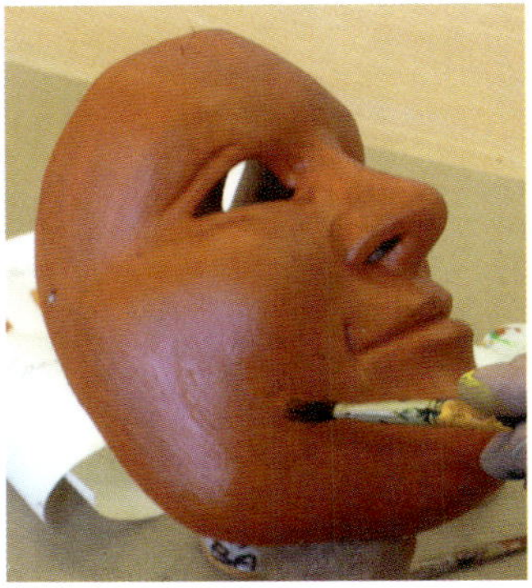

The base coat

Paint the darkest base tones of brown-beige all over the outside of the brown paper mask. Keep the colour just up to the outer edge – not too wet – and give it two layers to cover the surface entirely.

The second coat

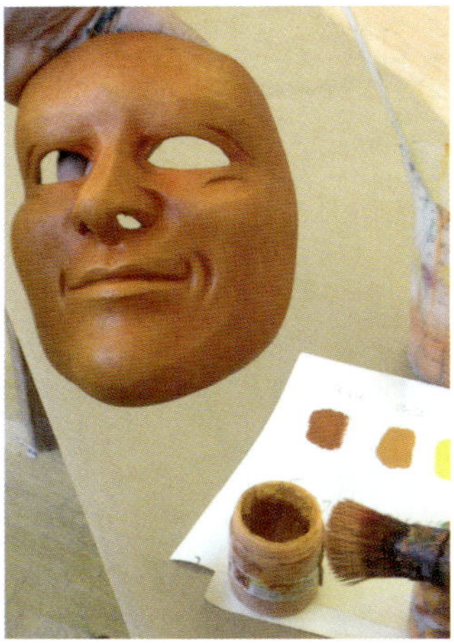

Dip the brush into the mid-range tone and wipe off any excess paint. Then lightly brush onto the high points of the mask. Build up a strong but gradual contrast, applying the orange-yellow colour minimally to start with, gradually extending it over the mask while still leaving as much of the dark base exposed.

The highlights

Painting with the lightest tones only cover the highest points of the mask, including usually the forehead, the eyelids, nose and lips. Get an even, symmetrical distribution of colour over the mask.

The mask is now ready for the last stage before wearing. Follow the processes outlined in Chapter 2 (pp 46–47) on how to varnish and, punch holes and attach elastic ready for fitting.

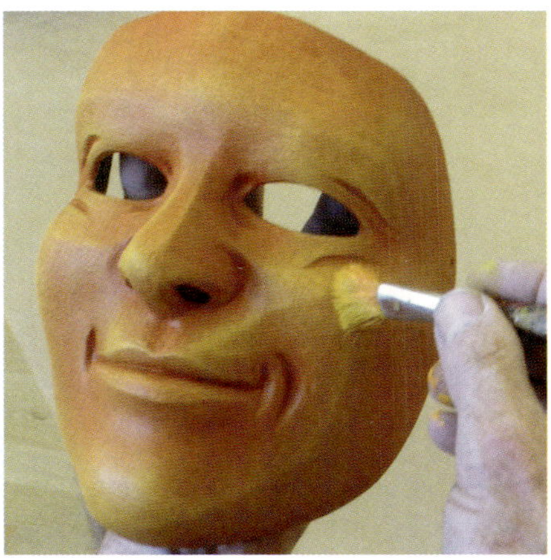

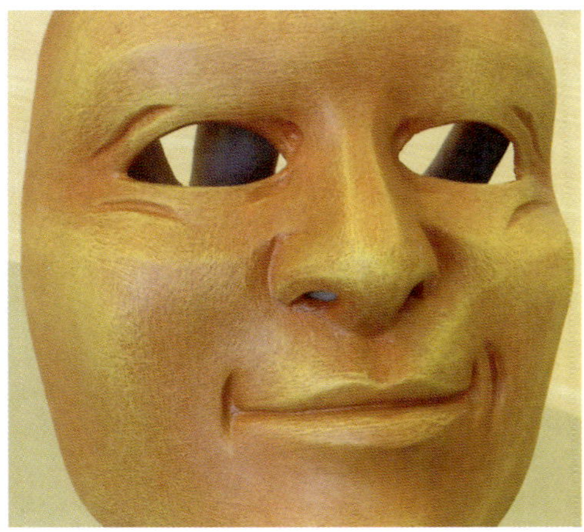

Designing and painting a choleric mask

Getting a feel for the mask

Observe a flame, a fire or candle and notice how heat, fuel and oxygen are required for the flame to live. It is heat of the body and the choleric muscle that drive the bold choleric temperament.

The list of all the words that come to mind on the theme of fire include: 'hot', 'burn', 'power', 'anger', 'temper', 'strength'. With these words (and whatever others you come up with) in mind, move in the quality of fire, finding the staccato, emphatic movement and the consuming quality of fire in your gestures.

Explore the interactive bodywork of pushing against resistance. With a partner stand opposite each other, front feet touching, and palms of hands in contact. Take it in turns to push each other, one of you offering resistance, so that the other can push against you. Take care not to suppress each other, but offer enough resistance to feel the power come up the back of the legs as they firm up to resist the pushing. Observe what this activity does to your facial muscles, what facial set becomes dominant? Using this experience go into drawing.

Drawing the Choleric

Your sketches will be invaluable when you come to complete the design, so try to get a feel for the temperament as you draw.

Body-line drawing

Take a red coloured pencil and drawing paper and draw the body, arms, legs and head in motion, continuously developing the image until a shape emerges that encapsulates the Choleric gesture.

Doodling the head and face

Scribbling in reds, bring out the muscular intensity of the fire and blood that the choleric embodies. Let this be playful but intense.

Front on and profile

For this process, once again draw two egg shapes, one upright and the other on an angle, about the size of a human head, and emphasise the willing and feeling zone of the head between the nose and jaw line.

Making a maquette

After you've shaped the clay into a ball, accentuate the lower willing area, allowing the fiery intensity to arise in the middle feeling area. The muscles are the bulging, tense places in the design, as are the forehead, the flaring nostrils, the tense firm mouth and the musculature in the jaw. Cholerics often grind their teeth down.

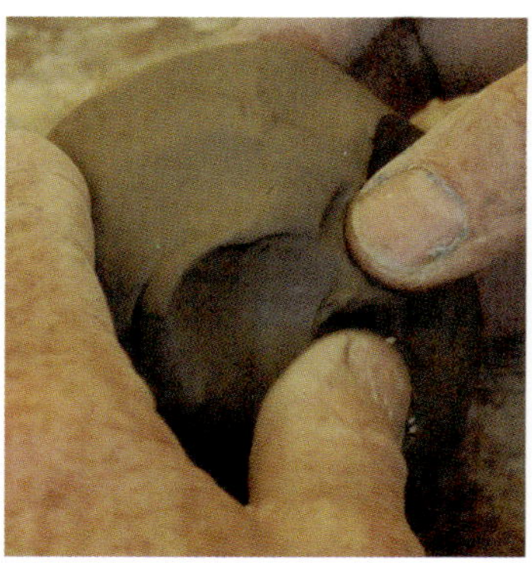

The full design

Get the reference material around you, along with a face cast on a board (see Chapter 2) and the small modelling balls of clay. Start by accentuating the muscles in the face, including the brow, nostrils and jaw. Finish with flesh around the lips and eyelids, always remembering to keep any clay by the plaster of the base in the eyes very thin, as it will be a constant indication of how the eyes of the wearer will make contact with the mask.

For designing a half choleric mask the following considerations can be helpful: take the top lip of the mask into the top lip of the face cast. Keep the lip line straight, sculpting it neither up nor down. Using the clay make a small tight lip with muscle tension creating a straight line from the centre of the top lip to the corners of the mouth. From the side of the lips on either side take the clay down onto the cheek a little, and then let it sweep up toward the ears.

Complete the mask on the clay design (see Chapter 2, pp 28–33) before painting.

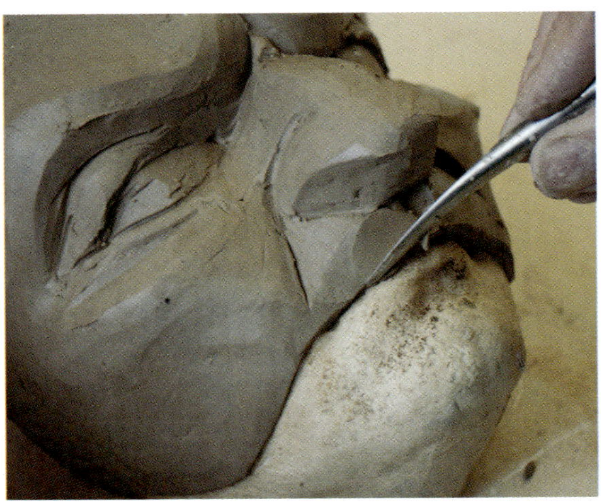

Painting the Choleric

Paint colours for the Choleric mask include: a raft of red and orange tones of acrylic paint from a deep dark red, a mid range of the same hue of red with orange, to go over the base coat, and a highlight of a lighter tone of orange with more white and yellow in it but similar in hue. It can help to mix a small quantity of the base coat into the mid range, and a small quantity of the mid range into the highlights to keep the hues similar.

Following the suggestions in Chapter 2 (pp 43–45), create a swab of the three deep red, mid-range and highlight tones, and see how they work together. You can add a little blue to cool down the base coat and play with orange for the mid-range tones. You may even want to use a little white for the highlights.

The base coat

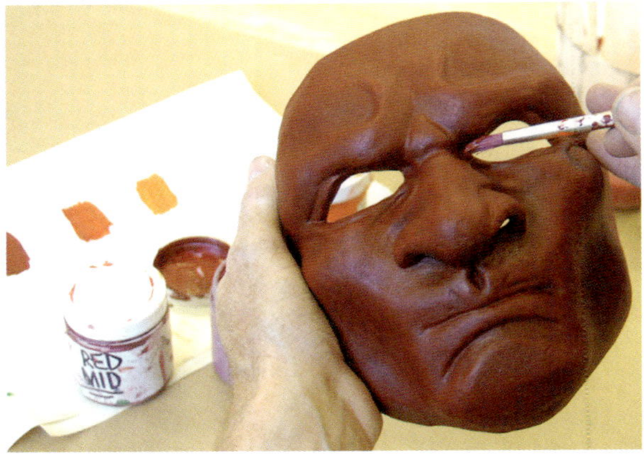

Paint the deepest tone all over the outside of the brown paper mask. Keep the colour just up to the outer edge without getting it too wet, and paint two layers to cover the surface entirely.

The second coat

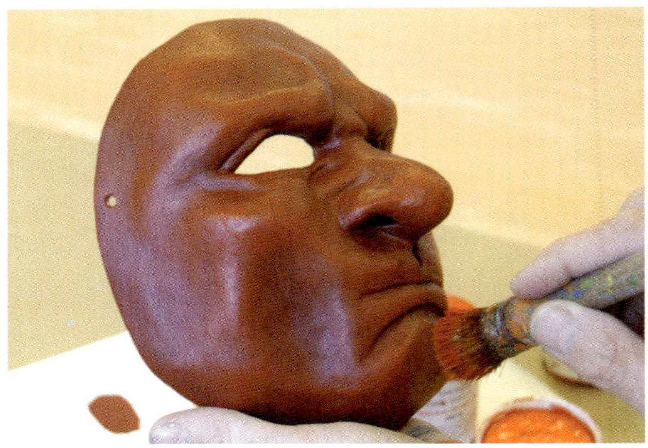

With the mid-range tone, dry-brush lightly onto the high points of the mask. Build up a strong but gradual, contrast. This is best achieved by applying the colour little by little to start with, gradually extending it over the mask while still leaving as much of the dark base exposed as possible.

The highlights

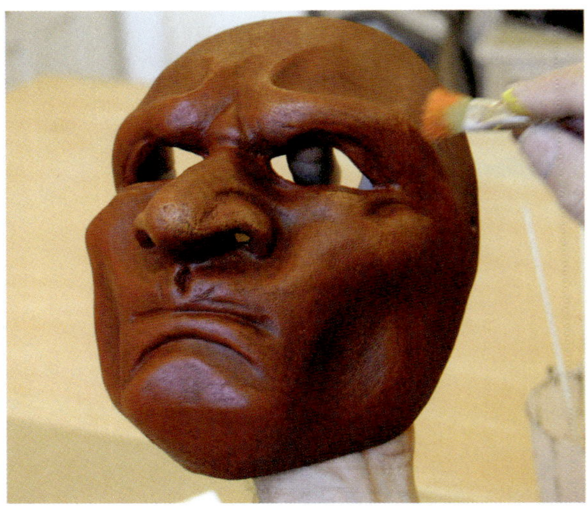

With the oranges and yellows, perhaps even a little white cover the highest points of the mask, including the forehead, the eyelids, nose and lips. Get an even, symmetrical distribution of colour over the mask.

Following the finishing procedures in Chapter 2 (pp 46–47), varnish and dry the mask and get it ready for fitting and wearing.

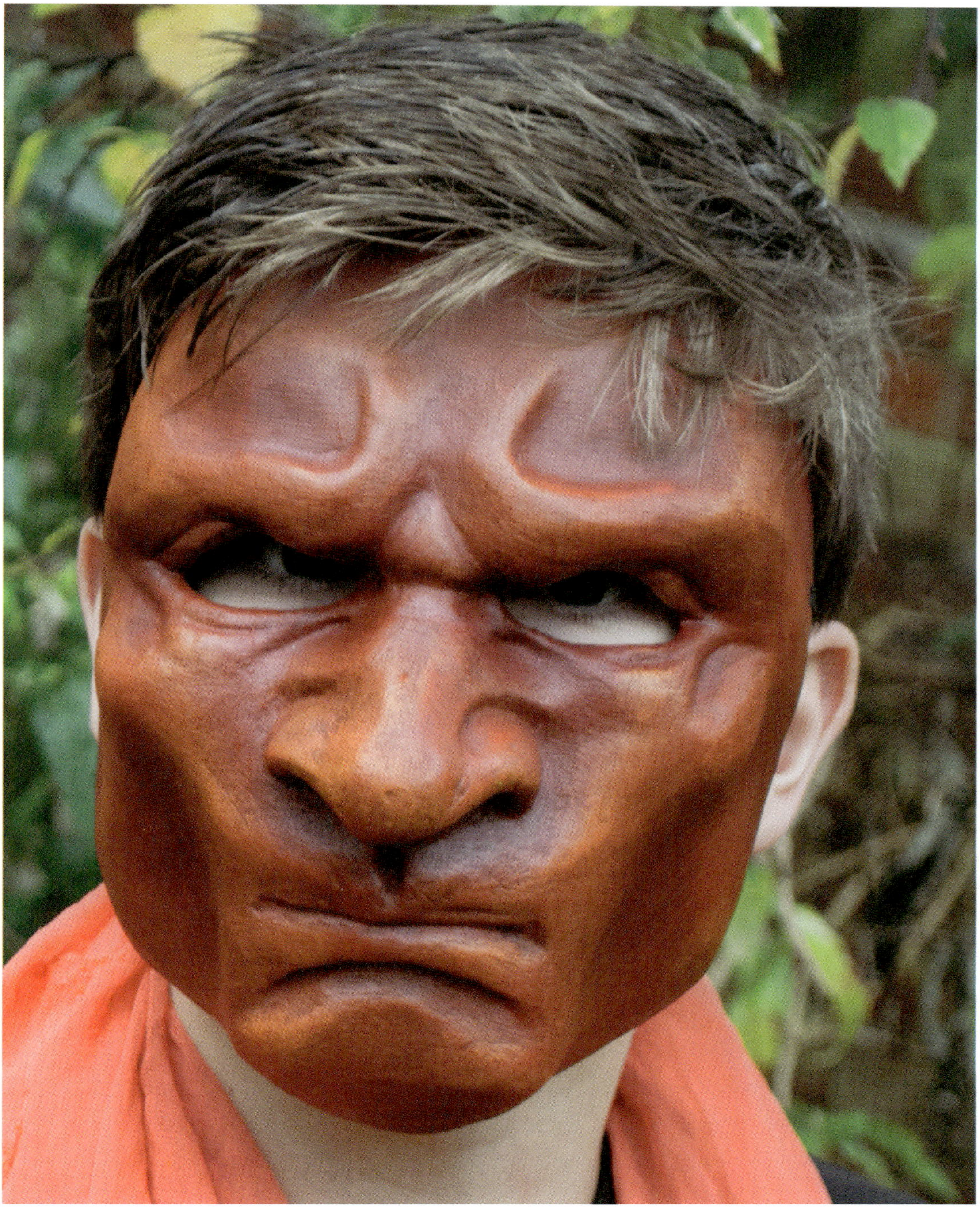

Designing and painting a neutral mask

Getting a feel for the mask

The neutral mask offers a place in between the four temperaments, a state that is not Choleric, Melancholic, Sanguine or Phlegmatic, but could be any one of the four if it was tipped in that direction. The neutral is neither old nor young, as in the Melancholic or Sanguine, neither is it male or female, or angry or bored, as in the Choleric and Phlegmatic respectively. The neutral is the most difficult to make as expression and temperament, mood and colour creeps in when you least expect it. Don't expect to make this mask quickly. However, when you have made a mask that is vaguely neutral, you will have made a significant step as a mask maker. As with the neutral body, which we will explore in Chapter 5, making a neutral mask is about letting go of the need to go into character and story. What makes the neutral mask an exciting challenge is the emphasis on holding back the urge to go to extremes, and finding a place of potential, both open and available. This is not lifelessness or a mechanical nature, but a vital openness and potential to go in any direction, though that step has not yet been taken.

The neutral exists between extremes, so what exercise is better than moving between the extremes of expansion and contraction. Working alone or with others, take a step forward towards the centre of an imaginary circle, contracting your body physically and imaginatively, taking up less space. Step backward to the start point and expand back to fill the space you occupied earlier. Now begin to take three steps forwards and with each step take up less and less space, becoming smaller and tenser like a nut. Go back to the middle where you started, taking up the original space you occupied, then move through that to the expanded position this time three steps backwards. By repeating this again, six steps forward into a contracted place, and then six steps back into an expanded state, you will be moving between extremes of big openness and contracted smallness. Find the middle place where you are neither contracted nor expanded. This is a neutral, balanced place where you could go in either direction but you don't.

Feel what is going on in the face and body. Write a list of all the words that come to mind on the theme of neutral, which often include: 'calm', 'balanced', 'focused', 'at peace', 'still', 'quiet'.

Then go into drawing.

Drawing the Neutral

Your drawings will be used as references when you come to complete the mask, so try to feel what you're observing.

Body line drawing

Draw a continuous line of the neutral body and, as with the temperaments, let it be spontaneous and fun, yet try to make sure that none of the temperaments find their way into the drawing – not the fiery tension of the Choleric, the erratic playfulness of the Sanguine, the painful deepness of the Melancholic nor the still broadness of the Phlegmatic. The idea being that the mask might potentially express all of them, just not at this point in time.

Doodling the head and face

Play around with the face, more like with the continuous line, going over the same form again and again, finding the mouth, nose, eyes chin and cheek bones until something neutral emerges. This is a meditation and could be seen as an exercise in looking for what needs not to be there, just as much as what does.

Front on and profile

Draw two egg shapes, one upright and the other on an angle, about the size of a human head, and find the balance of proportions between the thinking between eye line and the upper forehead, the feeling between the eyebrows and the top lip and the willing areas between the bottom of the nose and the chin and jaw. In this process one of the questions that arises is, how can the neutral be both human and neutral? This is your individual research.

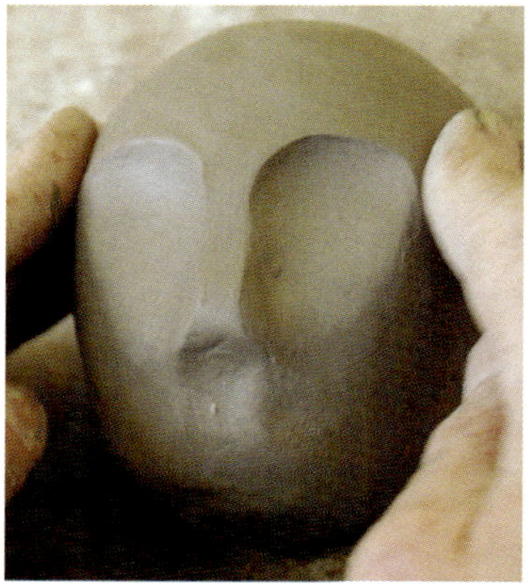 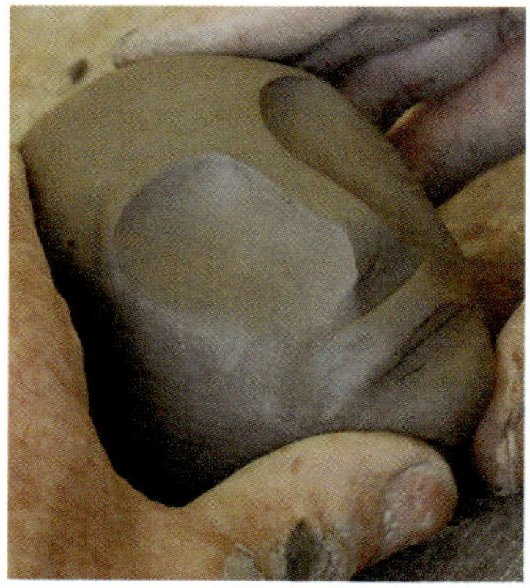 

Making a maquette

Take a round ball of clay in the palm of your hands, and squeeze it into an egg shape, without worrying about the detail. Create hollows where the eyes should be, draw the nose out and indicate the mouth. Taking some small, rolled-out pieces of clay, add them into the eye sockets to create eyelids and onto the lip area to create a mouth and gently work this in. You might need a few tries, taking a new ball of clay each time, so you can record your journey to something in the area of neutral. You will know you have got there when there is less background of story and character and more of an unknown quality about the maquette.

The full design

Gather the above reference material around you and place beside the face cast on a board (see Chapter 2 pp 28–33 for the face-casting process), along with small modelling balls of clay and begin to cover over any strong indications of character in the face cast. Add any clay to areas where a balance might be needed, for example more on the feeling between the eye line and the top lip and willing areas of top lip and chin and jaw, if the thinking part is dominant in the face cast and so on. Continue adding clay, but be careful not to enter into character and temperament, neither vacant nor mechanical. The neutral mask is not used for speaking, rather just for looking at centring and balancing the player and accentuating the body language.

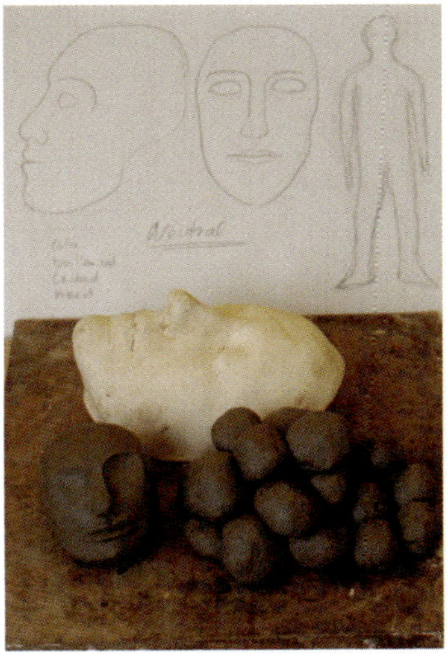

Painting the Neutral

Having finished the mask, and thoroughly dried it, add two tablespoons of diluted Polyfilla (as with the cow juice), into half a cup of white emulsion paint. This will thicken the paint and make it harder and easier to sand. I don't recommend any mid range or highlight on the neutral, but only three layers of white emulsion with Polyfilla. Once the paint and Polyfilla have dried thoroughly, rub the mask down with a fine sandpaper (180 is ideal), getting any lumps and bumps off that might tend towards character. Then paint it again twice (three times in total).

Having painted the three layers of white over the mask, take the opportunity to varnish it and punch the holes as described in the Chapter 2 (see pp 46–47). The mask is now ready for fitting and wearing.

Having made a mask of any of the four temperaments or Neutral is a step on a journey to making them all. My experience is that by making all of them you begin to find your own stamp and style. This will enable you to establish a series of gestures and planes in clay, and tones of colour in paint that will serve you in decisions you will have to make in creating masks in the future. As I've already suggested, in the western world the mask maker does not have many references to draw upon so the temperaments suggest a physical psychology that can enrich and inform any mask you design.

On a number of occasions I have used the temperaments as a direct reference to make masks for clients. Once for Trestle Theatre Company, a popular mask company from late last century, in a production they did called *The Island*, there were four characters that needed to play around in the periphery of the main action. As these four were described, one playful, another bored, the third slow and sad and the final feisty, I knew they were the temperaments. They became naive character temperaments.

In another instance, Pericles Theatre Company commissioned twenty-five masks and puppets for a production of *The Children of Lir*. There were four characters in there who each had a specific function which tallied exactly with the temperaments. The temperaments offer a mask designer a creative touchstone in how to interpret other characters. In the case of this production I painted the masks more lifelike than the strong primary colours of the temperaments, as this was more in keeping with the style.

In making all five masks, not only will you have a complete cosmology or family, but you will have a set that can work in many different contexts from performance to education, from therapy to self development. There is a demand for masks like this from all over the world and in many different contexts. The mask is a transitionary object, between the inner and outer world. The outer mask is created by maker; the inner world ignites when you put the mask on and breathe life into it through the body, voice and imagination.

Chapter 4

GENERAL MASK USING

Using masks invites the practitioner to step through an imaginary doorway from the mask-making studio into a space for performing, learning and therapy. With the creation of the mask, the outside has been completed; now the act of filling the mask from the inside, with the face, the body, the thoughts and feelings of the wearer begins. In this chapter I will consider various processes and exercises in preparation for wearing and using masks, including warming up the body, voice and imagination for the transformation required for filling the mask from the inside. I will consider some general principles and exercises in using masks and then explore more specifically the masks of the four temperaments. I will then give examples of how I have used the four temperaments in different fields and contexts.

General preparation for movement and voice with groups

The following exercises and processes are useful in preparing for the use of masks when working with groups – whether they're young adults, performers, members of a social therapeutic community or in a corporate setting. Some of these suggestions might be more specific to theatre practices but I include them here as the field is broad and these processes can be applied across different practices and contexts.

Golden hoop

To create an atmosphere of trust and openness in a group of people working together with masks, the golden hoop can be a very effective exercise to draw a group together and prepare them for using masks. As Michael Chekhov suggests, it can help establish a feeling of trust, safety and develop ensemble with a spirit of cooperation. (Chekhov, 1991) The image of the golden hoop is a picture of all the goodness and greatness that is contained within the group undertaking the project. All the positive qualities that each person has to bring to the group make up the richness of the golden hoop. At the start of each session, while standing in a circle, everyone is invited to reach up into the air and imagine that somewhere above the group is an imaginary golden hoop. The group is encouraged to bring it down and lay it at their feet all together in silence.

Laying the golden hoop on the floor in front of the group requires each person to go down on one knee (if they can make it) and place the hoop simultaneously on the floor. This is a position from which the warm-up exercises can begin.

At the end of the session this is repeated in reverse. The group reforms in a circle, reaches down in silence, picks up the imaginary golden hoop, which is now filled with all the content of the session, lifts it into the air with arms stretched out above, and simultaneously throws the golden hoop up into the air, in silence, for safe keeping. It has an accumulative effect and prepares participants for entering in and out of the masks and working creatively together.

Greek gym

When the golden hoop is placed at the feet of the group standing in a circle, the time comes to turn outwards to start the work of warming up the body and imagination more energetically. Mime exercises can warm up the body, using imaginative images rather than moving mechanically, which can prepare the group for working on speech.

One good mime exercise to begin with is the mime of washing off the everydayness of life and to prepare for entering a more imaginative sphere. Other activities to mime can be derived from events in the play. For example, using Shakespeare's *Pericles* as inspiration, we chopped down trees, from which we built the boat in mime.

The five Greek gymnastic events of running, jumping, wrestling, discus and javelin are the origins of the Olympic Games. In them, Steiner suggests you can find the sum total of all human gesture. (See Steiner, 1959)

The five mime exercises arising from the Greek gym are very invigorating.
They include:

- Throwing balls to each other – from the javelin
- Pushing in pairs – from wrestling
- Casting an imaginary net as if over the entire audience – from the discus
- Walking and running – from running
- Hopping and jumping – from jumping

Throwing balls

There are three main exercises for throwing balls. The first is in a group, where one ball is thrown between all the members of the circle. As the ball is thrown, the name of the person being thrown to is called out. The name should be called while the ball is in the air, not before it is thrown or after is it has been caught. This will become a principle for speech later on.

The second ball game is where the ball is thrown between pairs. Here the first thing to practise is throwing kindly and considerately: as the ball is caught, the catcher says, 'Thank you' to the thrower. The thrower then says, 'Pleasure'. The ball is passed back and forth in this way until it is evident that the rules are easy. Now the throwers are invited to do it without the ball but in mime. The pairs can be invited to have some fun at this point, throwing high and catching it from on high, rolling the imaginary ball across the ground and catching it on the ground and so on. It's important to remember to call the name of the person being thrown to as the ball is in mid-cycle through the air.

Pushing

This is done in pairs. Two people, fairly evenly matched in size, stand facing each other with their right feet touching at the toe. They place their hands out in front of each other, touching at the palms. Now with knees and elbows bent they begin to push slightly, back and forth. It is important that the movement in one direction is clear and carried through. Once this is established, the pusher is encouraged to take a step in the direction of the receiver, who takes a step backwards. This is repeated back and forth for a step at a time, and gradually increased to two and three steps. Now as the person pushing feels the resistance from the receiver, and they begin to move, they begin to make a deep sound, like a rumbling from the stomach. The receiver breathes in as they go backwards, and should be ready to make the belly sound when it is their turn to push. Once the three steps are complete, the sound stops and the receiver becomes the pusher. And so on. It's important to be careful not to hurt the voice while doing this.

Casting

This is best done by half the group facing the other half of the group, one half being an audience, the other being the caster. Ask the casting group to think of a fisherman or fisherwoman standing on a boat in the ocean with a circular net. The net is lying in the bottom of the boat behind them. It is useful to think of a coiled spring here as they bend down, pick up the net and unfurl with energy, as they fling it out in front of the fishing boat, as if over the entire audience.

What is important here is that while the net is flying through the air and covering the entire audience, the fisherman or fisherwoman has eye contact with the audience and stays arms outstretched until the net has covered all and has fallen into the sea. Then invite the group to bend down and pick up another net on the other side and repeat the casting. What is important here is that the tension from the coiled spring is released quite suddenly, and the prolonged moment of waiting for the net to land in the water is observed. This will be taken into speech later.

Running

Quite simply the group is invited to run in a circle, finding a speed that works for the group to keep going without overtaking each other. This means some runners will have to go slower than they would ordinarily go, while others perhaps need to move a little faster. When the running has been established, introduce the idea of gravity, pulling the runners down into the ground. Having done this, introduce the idea of levity, pulling them up, as if with a helium balloon. Now invite the runners to run between gravity and levity, not going completely into either. This is a challenging practice that can bring a balance to the group. It is important that the runners can do this walking if they are getting tired; what matters is that they participate wholly with both the gravity and levity so that head, feet, hands etc are all participating in each of the extremes. This will help them arrive eventually at a good balance.

Jumping

This is best achieved when participants stand in a circle facing forward. Invite the group to make a small jump of forty-five degrees to the left, and then back to the middle. Then invite them to do this to the right-hand side. Having done this a few times, increase the jump to ninety degrees, and invite them to jump to the left then in the opposite direction to jump back to face forward. This can be increased to three-quarters of a circle so that the jumpers, having jumped to the left side stop facing the person originally on their right. This can be repeated on the other side. Finally, for the really fit and energetic members of the group, invite those who feel confident to jump in a circle up to 360°, and jumping to the left they arrive back where they originally started, facing forward in the circle. It's important with this exercise that when they land they remain still. Whatever position they might be in is not important – if they are bent or on one leg, they need to remain still. This is good for balance in mask work and will be taken further in the speech exercises.

Speech exercises

Speech exercises, which have images and movement accompanying them, especially when brought in a fun and playful manner, are very effective in developing clear articulation and pronunciation. When imaginative movement accompanies speech, it can become rich in colour, variation and feeling.

With each of the mimed Greek gym exercises different principles of speech are developed, which have a natural feel without having to force the breath, analyse the larynx 'apparatus' or work mechanically. The following speech exercises have been devised by Rudolf Steiner.

Walking and running helps find the rhythm and meter in speaking, without stopping, or slowing down when the speaking needs to flow. By doing the physical movement of walking and speaking, each syllable of each word over the top of each step, the feeling of flow, metre and continuity begins to become apparent. Here is a simple series of sounds that can be spoken, one for each step, and repeated, elongating the 'm' at the end of each syllable to join it up to the next one:

Hum, Hem, Him, Hom, Hum

Different consonants can replace the 'H' to give variation, for example 'V', 'B' etc.

Throwing with speech

From throwing balls to each other, with the trajectory of throwing, flying, and catching, the speaker can be helped to imagine that the sounds exist before uttering them but are only audible for the moment of speaking. If we imagine a shooting star hurtling through space, invisible to the human eye, as it enters the earth's atmosphere it becomes visible through its fiery tail. As the mass is burned up it is no longer visible, but the remains continue down to the earth. So it is with the sounds in speech, they exist before and after we hear them, but only become audible when spoken through the larynx. The larynx does not produce the sounds, but makes them audible to the human ear. This is called speaking on the breath, which can be very supportive when using masks. When saying the following sequence of words, accompany each line with a gesture in mime of throwing a ball through the air. Speak the line beginning only when the ball is in the air and stopping when the ball is caught.

Fulfilling goes
Through hoping
Goes through longing
Through willing
Willing flows
In wavering
Whales in quavering,
Waves veiling
Waving breathing
In freedom
Freedom winning
Kindling

Having warmed up the speech by speaking on the breath so to speak, the following three processes of pushing, casting and jumping can be can be developed with the speech exercises at the end.

Pushing with speech

The exercise of pushing in pairs is derived from wrestling and supports the speaker by offering the resistance required for speech to come about. Through the pushing exercise, the speaker is encouraged to support each sound with movement, offering a physical response to accompany each word of the speech exercise.

Casting with speech

The casting a net exercise supports the speaker in communicating to the entire auditorium. By gesturing as if grasping the entire audience, the speaker can take the time to share their words with everyone sitting in the front, back, sides, or in the box if the theatre has one. This expansive gesture supports the clear, open articulation of words. When doing the gesture of casting in a group, the speakers are encouraged to speak it to the other half of the group sitting in different parts of the auditorium.

Speech exercises using the temperaments

Once you are warmed up, the following speech exercises begin to focus in on the temperaments:

Melancholic: *'Moisten mason mine essence.'*
Choleric: *'Come crooked craftiest cur.'*
Phlegmatic: *'By beaten bowers bide brave.'*
Sanguine: *'Lamer lightness, Leicester loiter.'*

General techniques of mask using

Whether using masks in performance, education or therapy, the mask has some common threads that can be summed up as follows: embodiment, transformation and energy. The mask offers the wearer a visual image comprised of a facial expression including lips, eyebrows and colour. These give the wearer indications of attitude and body architecture, which will help embody the feelings, character and archetype from a physical and emotional point of view. The mask is now like a narrow funnel for the wearer to communicate through, enhancing energy and focus.

Masks can support the development of larger-than-life archetypes by adding a constant cipher to maintain the power and force of the character, and allowing the wearer to come out of character very quickly when taking the mask off.

When using masks, the wearer's habitual body language changes, as he or she enters into the life of the mask. Even though masks can make the player feel empowered they also present a threshold: the mask is black inside and players can feel like they are in another place – a different world, far away. The following exercises and processes can help lead the wearer into the mask in a safe, spontaneous and authentic manner.

Finding the body and sounds to fit the face

Having done a warm up both physically through the Greek gym exercises and vocally through the speech exercises suggested, explore the following activities:

- Invite the group to move their eyebrows up and the mouth down. Keep the expression like that, as if fixed.
- Allow the breathing to change in order to keep that expression alive.
- Adjust the body to accommodate the feeling of the face by trying out different positions. For example, lift the shoulders and push the pelvis forward. Keep them like that.
- Explore making sounds that feel appropriate for this face and body configuration, if need be allowing sounds to turn into words.

Stop and drop the expression, the breath and body, and the sound and movement that was inspired by that face. Rub the face to give it a break. Repeat this a number of times until the group gets used to the idea that the facial expression can determine the kind of breath, rhythm, sound, gesture and body architecture that arises.

Mask rules

There are some important basic rules for the safety of all involved in using masks – for the wearers, the observers and facilitator. It is important that people always leave masks facing upright and not nose down, as this can chip the paint. Masks are best left on a table and not on the floor or a chair where they can be kicked and sat on. Believe me, this happens. Make a contract with the group that they can take the mask off any time they like, so they have control, and that they must take the mask off if you ask them to. In this way the group are invited to play and have fun, and they and the session leader have control in how far they can go. Masks can be very immediate and powerful, and so need to be respected and used in a disciplined fashion.

In order to demarcate a playing area for the masks to work in, put a rope on the floor about two meters in front of the audience. The mask players are then told not to cross that line.

Invite the players to choose a mask from a series of masks available on a table. When each person has chosen a mask that they feel drawn too, make sure the mask fits them. This is not always going to be possible because the masks are not going to be one size fits all. Pieces of foam are good to have nearby to pad out the mask if it is sticking into the eyes. Show the group how to put a mask on. The most stable way is to put one of the two elastics high up on the head and the other lower down, which stabilises the mask.

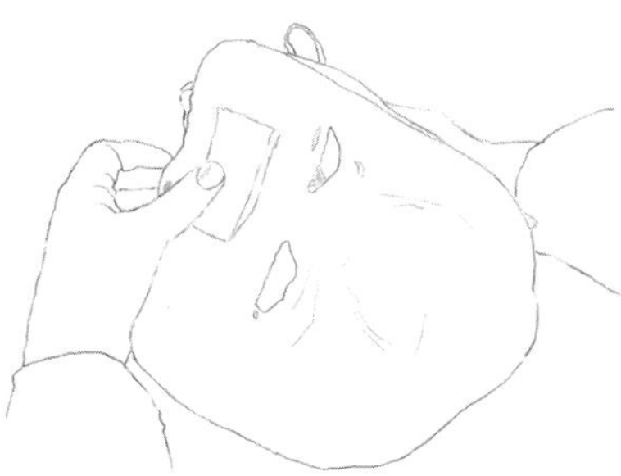

Filling the mask from the inside

The following process can be used with the temperament masks prior to identifying the masks as any particular temperament. This process is very helpful in finding out about a mask without knowing anything about its original purpose or function. Participants can work with their own mask, a temperament mask, or choose a mask made by another player.

Take a good look at the mask and adjust facial expressions, as much as possible to fit into the shape of those on the mask. By creatively interpreting each indication in the shape and features of the mask, the player can bring the mask alive by finding the congruity between the features represented in the lines, planes and contour of the mask and the bodily expression that it calls forth. This is like looking into a mirror, what you see in front of you is going to be you, soon.

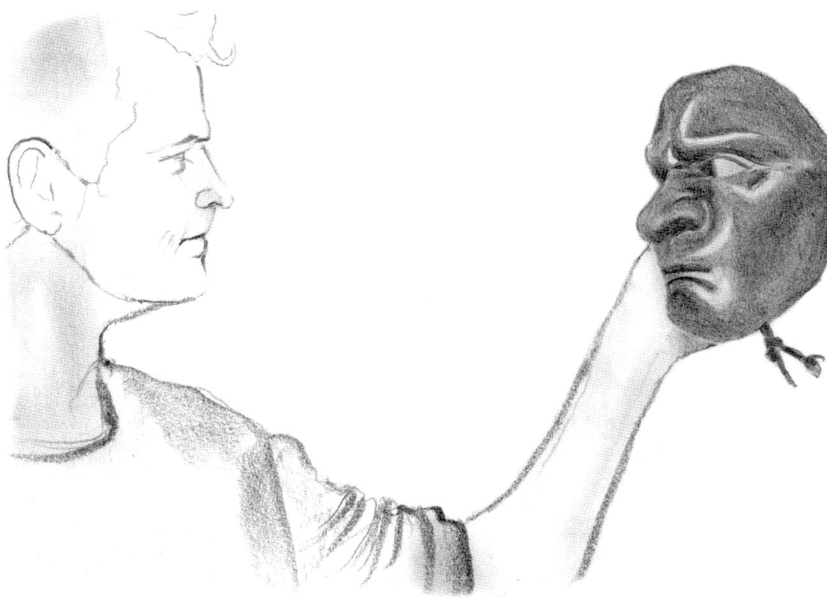

As with the face exercise earlier, explore how to fit the body into what the mask represents. Change your posture until it feels in tune with the face inspired by the mask.

Build up the sounds and movements as before, but this time, when the players are really transforming themselves into the masks, invite them to begin at the same time and to look out through the eyes of the mask. While doing this the players often

have an unexpected experience, something akin to looking at a pair of new glasses, and then looking out through them. It can affect the way the player sees the world, and so it should because they are now seeing the world through the eyes of a character of the mask.

Invite them to walk around as the mask, keeping the facial expression and body shape soft and light, but not forgetting what mask they have on their face. What is useful is to invite the mask players to imagine they are acting on a Richter scale from one to ten. One is the least extreme the mask face and body can be, almost no change to the player beneath, and ten is as extreme as they can go in face, rhythm and body. Having gone through the two extremes, suggest that they find a middle ground of five. This might be too much for some individuals who push themselves too hard, whereas others might need to take it high up the scale to really get a transformation.

The session leader can mirror back what they are doing in the mask. This will help the mask player to charge up the mask and amplify its life, and confirm that they are doing the right thing. This action of mirroring can act as a stimulation to the player who then amplifies their movement in the mask, which can make the masked players feel more at home in the mask.

Whatever size the group you're working with, split them in half and invite the one half to do the work in the mask and the other to watch. The ideal group would be twelve, then six could work first while the other six watch, following which the two halves will swap. In this way the mask players always have an audience to play to, and one can learn as much from watching as one can from being behind the mask.

Invite the players to interact with the other masks on the stage, greet them, see if they can find a little dance, or a common movement that each mask might do with another. Once each mask has met the other, ask them to stop still and turn their heads out and face towards the audience. This is an extraordinary moment, as the mask players encounter the audience for the first time. This element of real surprise is important to remember in a mask, as these are the moments of drama, where theatre is alive in the moment without a script or predetermined relationships.

Finally, because the players will have been in the masks for a few minutes by now, and will be getting face ache, invite the masks to stand in a line. Your relationship with the masked players is now more like a playful policeman, ordering them about and being playfully pushy.

A final element of play that can be really helpful is to invite the mask players to look out into the audience and to see if there is anyone they know there. If there is (which is not necessarily a given, although the mask player might pretend there is), invite them to wave at the person, who in turn will usually wave back.

Finally, invite the masks to take a bow, and turn with their backs to the audience.

This is a good time to take the masks off and to debrief the experience. Ask the players to sit down in front of the group and ask them how they feel. This is important for getting out of a role, as even though the masks are no longer on the players' faces, the residue of the experience is most likely still to be there as a physical and emotional tension.

These are questions you might ask:

- How did players feel in the mask?
- What did players enjoy?
- What did the audience see?
- What did the audience enjoy?
- What went well and worked?
- What did not go so well?

It is important to speak about what the masks did, and not to criticise. A good rule of thumb is: there are no mistakes, only differences. Then swap the group around, so audience now becomes the players and the players the audience.

Having introduced a number of exercises and processes for the general use of masks, all of which can be applied to all styles and traditions as a basic approach, I will in the following chapter focus more specifically on one of the themes of this book: masks of the four temperaments and the Neutral.

Chapter 5

USING MASKS OF THE FOUR TEMPERAMENTS AND THE NEUTRAL

Most of the exercises and processes outlined in Chapter 4 can be used with the full and half masks of the temperaments. The following mask-using sessions all use some of the same fundamental principles, processes and exercises but are aimed more specifically at the temperaments and the Neutral. They include specific images, interactive body work, vocal work with catch phrases and mantras, as well as improvisations.

Preparing and using the neutral mask

A mask teacher friend of mine calls the neutral mask the 'mask of unmasking'. It's a great term, as working with this idea highlights all our idiosyncrasies and makes our body language transparent, as if under a microscope. The neutral mask was developed by Jacques Lecoq in his mime school in Paris in the 1960s. He was inspired by the Japanese Noh mask Ko-omote, the virgin, which is poised between being and becoming, as if waiting full of potential for whatever life asks of it. The neutral mask heightens our attention on how we move, what attitudes we carry, consciously or unconsciously, like a mirror. By doing various exercises that bring the player into the present, in time and in space, more potential can arise for transformation. By being conscious of our body language we can be more free in choosing what movement, tensions and gesture we incorporate into our work. By becoming more in tune with 'being' instead of acting, we move, feel and speak more authentically. By being in the here and now, rather than thinking of the past or future, the actor becomes more alive and compelling. This is a great preparation for entering into the four temperaments, which are powerful and extreme states of being.

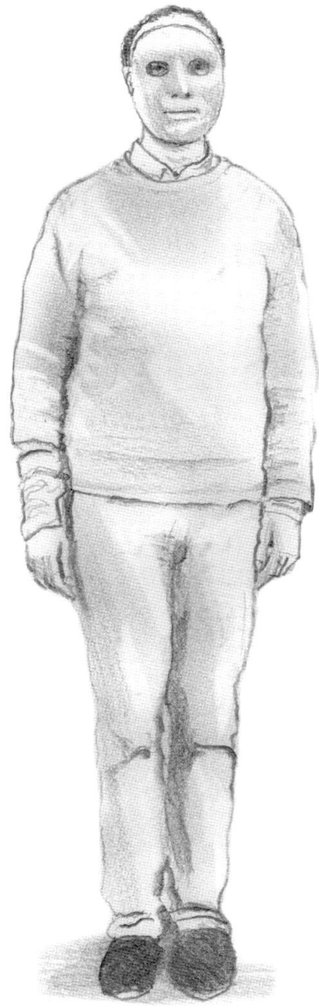

Preparing for the Neutral

Before looking at the neutral mask, here is an exercise to help players understand how one comes across with unconscious body language, so they have more choice when working with the neutral mask. The choices we have in how we move are derived from knowing what our natural tendencies are, what our unconscious body language is, including gestures, ticks and habits that we have adopted over the years. When we are conscious of these, we have more self-knowledge and so more freedom in managing our own physical behaviour and body language. This can help us clarify our own neutral state.

Copying each other walk

Having established the body language idea, invite the group to work in twos, giving each other feedback on what they notice in their body language through the following exercise. Participants should choose to be A or B.

Person A walks round the room, attempting to be as natural as possible. Person B observes them, initially in profile for a while, to observe how A leads. B must observe whether A leads with their head, the stomach, the pelvis or knees slightly in front. Having made these various observations, B follows in the footsteps of A, just two metres behind, getting in to their rhythm, and leading with the part of the body they have observed A lead with. Having practised this for a short while, B now begins to incorporate more of

the way in which A walks, including how A puts their feet down, the angle of their pelvis, how they swing their arms, turn their hands, the tilt of their neck – and so on.

Each of us is a riddle waiting to be unravelled and this is the opportunity to begin that process. Having undertaken this exercise for a few minutes, invite B to continue by asking A to do a number of tasks. Try asking them to do the following: sit down on a chair; stand up two or three times. B needs to try this as well to see if he or she can slip into the skin of A. Ask A to do other things, such as running over to the window and looking out. Invite B to copy how A ran and looked out of the window, and any number of activities that you think will give them a better idea of how A moves.

Having observed and tried out the various rhythms, mannerisms, actions and gestures of A, the latter can now sit down. B now gives them a show of what they have observed. I call this 'home movies.' If there are enough neutral masks to go round, the Bs can put them on for this part.

A watches how they are manifested in B's demonstration, and B takes little pauses in what they are playing back for A, as if to say, 'This is what I saw you do.' Having done 'home movies' for a few minutes, B stops and they give each other feedback.

Feedback can include A sharing with B what they recognised about themselves in B's playback. A needs to feel free to accept what B has offered of themselves as valuable or not. This can be confronting but it can also be revealing and very insightful. B can feed back to A where they felt A in their body. To finish off, B needs to 'brush off' the tension that they have taken on through the mirroring exercise, as if dusting off the snow having walked in from the cold, or drying after a shower.

Exchange the favour, or as someone said, time for revenge. It is however important that this work is undertaken with an attitude of respect and collaboration.

Having explored the individual body language of members of the group, it is time to refine the experience of neutrality.

Neutrality may be described as a state where the self resides beyond the idiosyncrasies of character.

The following processes can prepare the mask player in finding their vertical, neutral 'ego-experience'.

Fast and slow

This exercise is designed to help a neutral tempo by exploring the sagittal plane of space concerned with movements left and right. Invite the group (any number of participants between six and eighteen, twelve being the best) to sit down on a chair somewhere in the room. Then ask them to pick up the chair and move across the room, where they put the chair down and sit on it again. Encourage them to go as fast as they can without running, taking care not to bang into anything or anyone. Tell them that the last person to be sitting is a rotten egg. When they have completed their first walk, ask for feedback about their experience: usually this will harvest responses that it felt dangerous, fun, fearful, chaotic. Then ask them to move again, applying the same rules as before, but this time as slowly as they can with everything – walking, picking up and sitting down, this time, the first one being the rotten egg.

When they eventually come to sitting, get the group's feedback from having participated in the second exercise. Common reflections included that it was 'focused', 'intense', even 'boring'. Finally invite the group to repeat the same actions with the chair but this time they must be sure not to move fast or slow. By keeping themselves in check they are not rushing or slowing down, but keeping themselves balanced between fast and slow, and so they can begin.

Feedback can express various responses – perhaps that it felt 'normal', 'calm', 'balanced', 'natural', that there was 'time to breathe', even 'neutral'. Ask each of them to remember their own particular feeling and continue on to the next exercise.

Expanded and contracted

This exercise is about taking up space by imagining you can radiate out and become large, or contract your aura and become small. This exercise explores the plane of space of forward and back, namely the frontal plane. Invite the group to stand in a circle with their hands on their hips and elbows touching. Each individual occupies an equal amount of space. Ask them to drop their arms to their sides and take a step backwards. As they do so, invite them to imagine that they are filling the space between themselves and those standing at each side of them in the circle. By filling the gap, they have to imagine getting bigger and radiating outwards in all directions. Invite them to enjoy their big-ness. Step back to the start point, reducing the amount of space they are taking up, so as not to encroach on the personal space of those next to them. Now ask them to take a step forward towards the centre of the circle, again being mindful of not encroaching on the others. By contracting their bodies physically and imaginatively, they will take up less space. Ask them to step backward to the starting point and expand back to fill the space between those on either side. Repeat this again, next time taking two steps outwards and expanding to the fill a bigger space, then back to the starting point. Then forwards two steps and contracting even more. Then three steps out, becoming giants; invite them to imagine they are waving their arms in the air and moving the clouds about, as big as giants. Then wave goodbye and return to the starting point. Then having passed though the middle start point and moving three steps inwards, imagine becoming so small that the whole body becomes tense and tightly contracted into itself as if participants can't touch each other for fear of intruding. Then

moving between one extreme of being expanded through to the other of being contracted a number of times, invite the group to find their own middle point. Ask them to be aware of the middle point between being expanded and contracted and invite the participants to break the circle and walk around the room criss-crossing, and when there is a gap, move towards it, and maybe change direction. Encourage them to greet each other as they walk around, and eventually to come to a stop. Asking what the experiences of this state between expanded and contracted felt like, the comments might include: 'focused', 'balanced', 'calm', 'centred', 'in myself'.

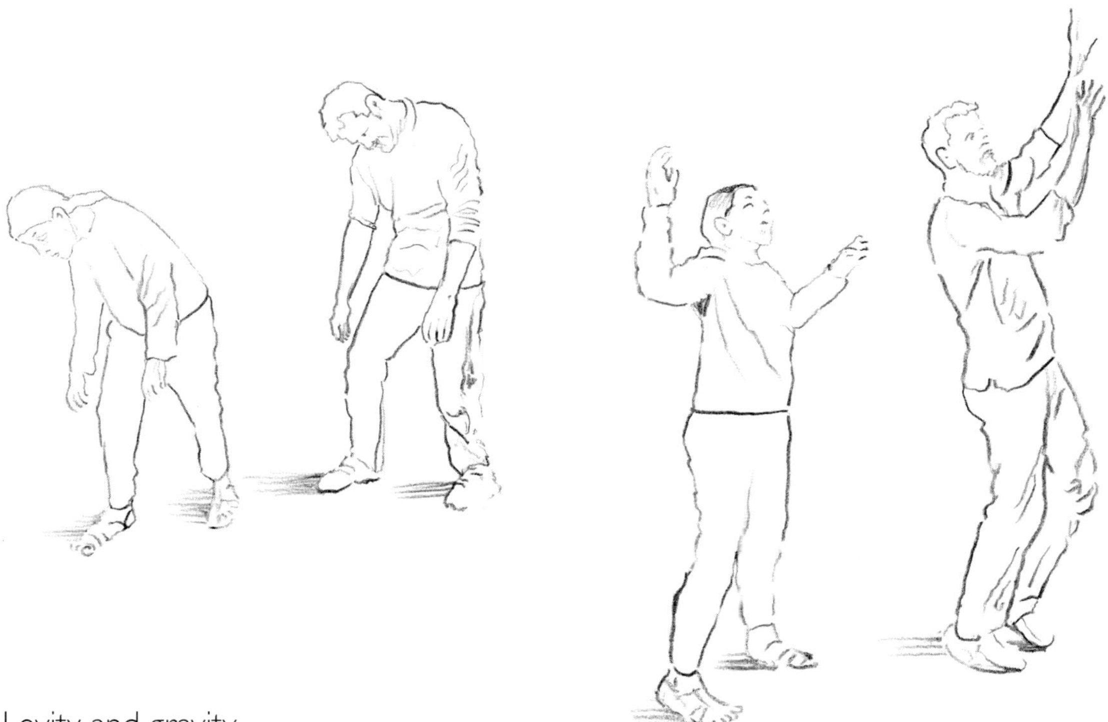

Levity and gravity

This exercise assists in exploring the horizontal plane of space and finding the middle between up and down. Standing in a circle, invite the group to face the person on their right. Ask them to feel the weight of their body, as if gravity was pulling them down towards the earth. Describe it as if their skeleton is weighing them down and making them feel heavier. Ask the group to begin walking around in a circle, allowing each step to be an effort, as if they had been walking through the desert without water for days and were about to drop to the ground. After walking the circle twice, invite the group to turn and face the person behind them.

Now ask them to feel as if there is very little gravity, as if they were about to take off and float up into the air. Invite the participants to imagine they are being pulled up by the top of the head, as if the heavens were pulling them off the ground. Encourage them to walk on their toes, lightly, eyebrows up, a smile on their faces. Let them walk around in the circle, allowing the levity of the experience to carry them, head up and looking skyward. Having walked the circle twice, ask them to come to a stop.

The point now is to invite the individuals to move through the experience of gravity, gradually lightening and rising up through the start point and continuing up into the experience of levity a number of times on their own. Like playing the scale of an instrument, ask them to go up and down until they begin to find a middle point where they are not light or heavy, but somewhere in the middle. At this point invite the group to walk around and greet each other and come to a stop.

Feedback can illicit statements such as: 'I feel in control', 'balanced', 'centered'. Let this be a reference for the neutral experience that can be taken into the neutral mask. All three of these processes can be used together, or if time does not allow, use one or two as a reference for entering into the mask.

Using the neutral mask

Hold up the neutral mask and ask the group what they see. I have often heard: 'not old or young, male or female, happy or sad, but poised in a state of becoming.' The neutral mask can have different connotations for different people, some quite disturbing, as the mask is white and has no eyes looking out from it yet.

Thrust of the mask

Having demonstrated how to put the mask on, with elastic in the correct place above the ear, one higher the other lower to stabilise the mask, invite the players to break the ice. Ask the two players to stand four metres away from the audience, back to the audience, and invite them put on a neutral mask each, checking if they need foam to help the fit. Help them to find the references of neutral from the previous exercises, of levity and gravity, expanded and contracted. Ask one of them to turn around and briefly look

at the audience taking in each audience member with their eye contact. Ask the mask to walk towards the audience until somebody in the audience says stop. Ask the audience to be honest in saying, 'Stop' when they feel the mask is close enough. This can be different for each member but ask them to come to an agreed distance.

What usually occurs it that depending on the individual body language in the mask, they will be asked to stop at about 2 metres (8 feet) away from the audience. This is because the mask has a thrust, or projection, with which the audience is happy, and beyond which the presence of the mask becomes overpowering or in some cases frightening and intimidating. Ask the second mask to do the same thing as the first, to approach the audience until they say stop.

Body language

The body language of each individual is very different, albeit unconscious. This is the extraordinary nature of masks, the neutral in particular. Give two people exactly the same mask and it reveals different things about the wearer. The neutral mask is like a microscope. The wearer's body is highlighted and becomes accentuated, more so than unmasked. As the face of the individual is no longer there to read, and its subtle indications of emotion, the body tells the audience what is going on. What is unconscious becomes highlighted, and now is the chance to give each other feedback, by becoming aware of unconscious body language, we have more choice in the way we communicate with our bodies. Feedback needs to be given in constructive ways, as each of us has different body language, which is determined by many factors. These can include how the body has taken on psychological factors from upbringing, family, education, accidents and trauma.

Invite the two players prepared in the masks to perform a number of activities that help to make body language understandable. These are some observations and interpretations that have been made, which may give you an idea of what to focus on.

- Feet out, heels together
  This can give an impression of being very open and available
- Chest out, pelvis back
  This can give a feeling of someone stifled, struggling
- Head down, while looking up at audience
  This can suggest menace
- Head up, while looking down at the audience
  This can give an impression of arrogance as well as fear
- Hands in front, holding fingers, with feet slightly in
  This can give an impression of low self esteem

Having established some of the neutral mask's rules and idiosyncrasies, it is time for them to meet each other. The following exercise is great for exploring relationships without telling stories too quickly, but staying open to the unknown for as long as possible.

Crossing in twos, one step at a time

This exercise was taken from John Wright, who tells me he was inspired by films of the Fratellini Brothers' clown show and can help to work with the playfulness and technique of the mask in relationship to the creative impulse of the actor, the relationship between two actors on the stage, and the third relationship with the audience. By keeping these three relationships alive in any moment, the neutral mask invites us into the world of mask theatre.

Invite the group to divide into two halves and face each other across a room in two straight lines. The facilitator stands down at the bottom to be an audience. Choose one row to be A and the other B. All in group A look out at audience while taking a step toward B, which is focusing on A. When A looks at B, this is the cue for those in B to turn their heads towards the audience. While looking out at the audience, the whole of B now takes a step towards A, which is looking at B. And so gradually, step by step, A and B get closer and closer to each other. As they do, the tension gets more and more intense.

What is important here is to emphasise that these two players (A and B) have no past or future together; rather, as with neutral, they are open and interested in each other. Many stories can begin to develop as the pressure of getting closer intensifies. Encourage the members of the group not to go into the stories, but to keep doing the exercise, seeing how close they can get to each other without invading their mutual space, putting their hand on each other's shoulders, and, if really focused, sitting down together. The piece can be left here, or if the group feels confident, they can return back to where they came, still playing the game of moving one at a time while the one being still, offers the focus to the mover.

Now for the mask. Invite two volunteers up to put on a neutral mask. Have them stand about 8 metres (26 ft) apart, or on the opposite sides of the room. Have them face the wall, with their backs to each other. When they are calm and focused, invite them to turn round to face each other wearing their masks and of their own accord to spontaneously perform the exercise just practised.

From the point of view of the individual, this piece is a powerful demonstration of the living triangle of relationships between the creative impulse of the one person, the other mask on the stage and the audience. This can become an example of good masked theatre. Jacques Lecoq and other mask teachers have many other exercises for the neutral mask, which can be found in courses and published literature. The important thing about using the neutral in relationship with the temperaments, is that it offers a calm centre from which to go into the extremes that the temperament masks occupy.

The masks of the temperaments

In working with masks of the four temperaments we can see extreme and unbalanced aspects of any one individual. They are not balanced, decent, kind and considerate, but hold a position of contrasts that can be rich, funny and disturbing. The mask is unchanging, as it holds a moment caught for eternity for us to look at and explore. This is also the genius of the mask, as it offers us the opportunity to explore extremes, to get to know them in the safety of a workshop, classroom space, and to try things out in the here and now. The following is an exercise that can introduce the masks to a group in a playful and creative way.

Blind masks of the full temperaments

Having established a neutral space of calm, rest, openness and focus, you are now going to encourage the players to move into the extremes of the temperaments. One at a time, using full masks of the four temperaments, invite a volunteer to stand in a neutral attitude and close their eyes. Then put a mask on them: looking out through the eyes of the mask, the wearer must figure out who they are by looking at the group

mirroring them back. The question the wearer in the mask has as they look at the audience is: *Who am I?*

Keeping a neutral attitude, the wearer looks out at the others standing in front of them and tries to find out who they are by copying the body language that the audience is mirroring back to them. This piece requires that the audience looks at the mask and imagines what body shape and gesture it needs in order to be embodied. The wearer copies the movements and gestures of each person and gradually builds up a moving sense of who they are. After a number of minutes the group offering the mask indications of who the wearer might be stops and watches; the person in the mask plays back all they can remember from what they have seen. After the playback has been completed, invite the mask player to close his or her eyes, go back to a neutral feeling, and take the mask off. Give them the mask to see.

It is a useful process of getting to know the masks of the four temperaments, by warming up to the embodiment of the archetypes through spontaneous interactions with members of the group.

Introducing the world of the temperaments

Understanding takes place when we reflect upon experiences. The experiences we encounter awake in us new levels of being which have to be integrated. As we make meaning of them afterwards the penny can often drop.

In this chapter we will explore different levels of experience, and the learning gleaned through reflecting upon these experiences. We will explore three different experiences. Firstly imagination which takes us into qualitative feelings, then into bodily experience awakening the will, and finally the spoken word taking us into our thinking. The combination of these three can offer the opportunity of entering holistically into the experience of each temperament, culminating in the mask.

Preparing and using the melancholic mask

The four elements are the roots of the four temperaments, giving them their particular signature. The Melancholic, connected to the earth, feels the predominance of the skeleton, the physical structure of the body. This enables the Melancholic to experience the physical body so strongly.

Entering into the imagination of the earth element

Standing with a group in a circle, invite them to imagine that before them is solid rock. Invite them to name some of the qualities that they imagine in this rock: 'hard,' 'dense', 'heavy,' 'solid' and so on. With each participant having contributed something to the image of rock, invite the group to step into this 'imagination 'and to take on the qualities of rock. Encourage them to feel the resistance and gravity of rock, the weight upon their shoulders. Encourage them not to fight the resistance but rather to submit to the density of the imagination, and to allow their bodily movements rhythms and gestures to express the idea of rock. The movement will become slower, as the struggle to move continues.

Invite them now to work on the out breath, even shaking the head a little as they walk round the room passing each other with a sigh. These gestures help to capture the struggling, victimised attitude of being a Melancholic. The final movement needs to be of a human quality, not exaggerated purely with the idea of the element.

To conclude, stop the movement, and ask the individuals for feedback regarding how they experience the exercise. Was it familiar? How did it make them feel? Did they find it excruciating and as far away from their natural disposition as possible? Did it remind them of anyone they know, friends or family?

Experiencing the melancholic body

This exercise helps to experience more intensely in the body what was experienced as an image and also movement. This time, the physical resistance is offered to invoke the feeling of what this extreme might be like. The following exercises are best demonstrated before inviting participants to join in. In order to take care of people's needs and tendencies to overdo it, tell the group to only get involved as much as they feel their bodies can take. Older people can do less of this work, whereas younger people need more of it and enjoy it more.

The image that accompanies this exercise is of the old woman or man walking up the hill from the shops carrying two heavy shopping bags, one in each hand. The bags weigh the person down, dragging the shoulders down, the walk is slow and painful.

In groups comprising of three people (A, B and C), suggest the following: A takes the first turn and stands in the room in a neutral attitude. B sits on the floor behind

A, taking A's wrists in their hands, holding on as if there were shopping bags in each of A's hands. A begins to walk slowly, dragging B along on the floor behind. If, after a few steps, A begins to rush and fight, C offers some more resistance by putting their hand on the back of A's head. By pushing their head down, the experience of submitting to the yoke becomes more evident. Having crossed the room, or a number of metres, stop and exchange the experience so A, B and C have all had a turn. It is possible to have two more people involved in this piece of interactive body work, one to take each of the legs by the ankle. This gives the added experience of the 'ball and chain', which can really take you into the melancholic experience of having to overcome life's hardships.

Having completed the exercise, and each participant having had the experience, including feedback of the experience, invite participants to re-create the experience they had while being held back by the others in the small group, but this time without the resistance from the others. Invite them to find the resistance, weight, head down, shoulders sagging and walk around the room at the same time. Ask them to greet each other in the manner of a rock/earth person. Now they will be getting into the rhythm and disposition of the Melancholic and are ready for the following mantra.

The spoken mantra for the Melancholic

With the imagination and bodies of the group members now fully warmed up to the melancholic disposition, introduce the mantra. A mantra is a sound, word or phrase that is repeated over and over again in order to instil a specific quality in the speaker. Mantras can be spoken silently or aloud, but are primarily, in this instance, only triggers for the speaker to remind themselves of what they are habitually thinking. The mantra is a voice in the head of the individual that helps keep in touch with the mask which they will inhabit shortly. The mantras given in this book are only indications of what

I have arrived at over the years; however, these can be changed and tweaked when necessary. Try these out and see if they work:

- A mantra for the immature Melancholic: *'I am all alone, nobody understands me.'*
- For the more mature Melancholic the mantra could be: *'No pain, no gain.'*

Invite the group to say the melancholic mantra aloud to themselves, while keeping the bodily gesture they have discovered from the previous exercises. Invite them to say the phrase to each other, as if it is the only words they can use. After a while, ask them to say it silently to themselves, while greeting each other. Now each player is ready to put on a mask.

Meeting the melancholic half mask

Make a contract with the group before beginning this piece that reminds them of their freedom to join in or not. This is one step further from the 'blind mask' exercise where the wearer does not know that the mask looks like. Here they do know, but they do not have much time to look at the mask, rather they have to keep the mantra, body and imagination from the previous exercise alive and keep doing what they were doing without the mask on.

The contract is: *If I ask you if I can put a mask on you, you can say no, and I will ask someone else. If you are happy to have the mask on, keep doing what you were doing without the mask on. If you want to stop at any point you are free to do so, and if I ask you to stop, you need to do so and take the mask off.*

When you have their agreement, begin.

While looking at the group embodying and interacting with this temperament, find someone who is doing it effortlessly, as if they might be of the temperament themselves. Invite them to put the mask on, making sure it fits. Be sure to offer them some foam if it is poking into their eye. As the mask begins to move around the room, greeting the others, ask those who are not wearing a mask to stop, and to find their way back to neutral. Encourage the mask wearer to keep a distance, although the distance for a handshake is often acceptable, especially if the mask is asked to greet a number of the others.

At this point the group usually stops and is entranced by the mask figure embodied in the melancholic temperament half mask.

When the mask has had the opportunity to greet each member of the group, ask them to stand still, close their eyes, and draw themselves up to their full height. Then help them to take the mask off and show it to them. This is time for the feedback.

- What did the mask wearer experience from within the mask?
- How did the others experience the mask in the room?
- What was easy, what was difficult?
- Was this familiar, or not?

Having debriefed the experience, invite everyone to take an imaginary shower, washing off the earthy, blue experience of the Melancholic, and help them to arrive back at a more neutral version of themselves.

Preparing and using the phlegmatic mask

The watery element is what lies at the root of the phlegmatic temperament. Water in its natural state takes the shape of the vessel it is contained in, whether that be a glass, a pond or a lake. It is only when water is acted upon by the force of the other elements that we get the waves in the ocean from the wind the moon, or the steam in a geezer, or the silt in a river pulled down to the ocean by gravity. The natural state of water is still.

Entering into the imagination of the phlegmatic element

Following the indications from the earthy Melancholic, one can develop words for the Phlegmatic. Standing with a group in a circle, invite them to imagine that before them is a well or a deep pond. Invite them to name some of the qualities that they imagine in the water before them: 'still', 'deep', 'transparent', 'filling the container' and so on. When each participant has contributed something to the image of water, invite the group to step into this 'imagination' and to take on the qualities of water. Encourage them to feel the resistance of water, far less than rock, but more than air. Ask them to feel the weightlessness of floating in water, the flowing form of movement that this engenders. Warn them against whipping up a storm, but encourage them rather to submit to the image of the stillness of the water, and to allow their bodily movements, rhythms and gestures to be in the quality of a slow flowing water being. The movement will become slower and more lethargic as the idea develops.

Invite them now to work on the balance between the in and the out breath; invite them also to blink their eyes slowly and enjoy the feeling of being, rather than doing. It is important for the water person that they can feel pleasure in being in the here and now in a calm, supported manner. As with the Melancholic, the nature of the movement needs to be incorporated into the natural body gestures of the player rather than being something they have taken on and are externally representing.

Experiencing the phlegmatic body

To help experience the phlegmatic in the body, interactive body work involving floating is most effective. There are a number of experiences that a small group could give an individual if you have the support and confidence. Here are a number of suggestions. It is important to consider the threshold some of these exercises might present, and adjust the experience accordingly. For example, some people are fine with being picked up and carried by the group, whereas another might find this needs too much trust letting go. The following exercises are best demonstrated before inviting participants to join in.

The image that accompanies this exercise is of floating in the Dead Sea, where the salty water gives one more buoyancy and support. This is effortless and relaxing and feels pleasurable. That's the feeling we need to engender, anyway.

In groups of six, each person, one at a time, has the opportunity to be supported in the following way: the first person to take a turn to lie down on the floor, or sits on a soft chair without any arm rests in a neutral attitude. The other five take up positions kneeling around them, one at each of the legs, arms and head.

One at a time, starting with a leg, the supporter puts a hand under the knee and ankle, and slowly takes the weight of the leg. There can be a struggle for some people to let go, and they need reminding to try at least to trust and give their weight to the carrier. After a moment when the first leg is floating, repeat the same thing with the second leg. When supporting the arms, take the elbow in one hand and wrist in the other. Be sure to keep the movements slow and rhythmic, and not to let them get chaotic. Finally ask the fifth member of the group to take the head in both hands, taking care not to cover the ears, allowing the head to float the head gently. Now all five limbs, the head as the fifth, are floating together.

Calm, soothing sounds can support the experience. For example, humming like the parent rocking the baby rhythmically in the cradle, or bubbles popping in water.

When the first person has finished their experience, invite a second person to lie down. If the group around the floater move to change the limb they were carrying, less tension will be brought into the exercise. The person who had been floated takes the last limb, as they need a moment to digest and integrate the experience before going into activity.

When everyone has had a turn and the exercise is complete, take a moment to hear any feedback. Now invite them to recreate the experience they had without the support from the others. While standing, encourage the group to feel supported and weightless, as if they were being carried. When they have got into the rhythm and disposition of the phlegmatic, they are ready for the mantra.

The spoken mantra for the Phlegmatic

With the imagination and body warmed up to the phlegmatic disposition, introduce the mantra, seeing first if they work for the group:

- A mantra for the Phlegmatic: *'I like things just the way they are.'*

This I find suffices for both the mature and immature Phlegmatic.

While keeping the state bodily gestures they have discovered from the previous exercises, invite individuals to say this phrase initially to themselves, then to each other, as if it is the only words they can use. After a while, ask them to say it silently to themselves, while greeting each other. Now somebody is ready to put on a mask.

Meeting the phlegmatic half mask

When approaching an individual who has encapsulated the temperament, remind them to keep the mantra, body and imagination going, now with the mask on. Be sure to offer them some foam if necessary and when you have their agreement and they are comfortable let them begin. Remind the group of the contract (see p 110).

As the mask moves round the room greeting the others, those who are not wearing a mask need to be reminded to stop what they are doing and find their way back to neutral.

As the group stops and observes the masked figure embodying the phlegmatic temperament, be aware of the energy in the room. This is usually calm, relaxed and still. When they have greeted everyone, ask the mask wearer to stand still, close their eyes and draw themselves up to their full height, close their eyes and find a neutral state. Then help them to take the mask off and show it to them. This is time for the feedback.

- What did the mask wearer experience from within the mask?
- How did the others experience the mask in the room?
- What was easy, what was difficult?
- Was this familiar or not?

The reflections often include: 'calm' and 'balanced', 'introverted' and 'in the present'. Having debriefed the experience, invite everyone to dry off the watery experience of the phlegmatic and bring them back to more neutral version of themselves.

Preparing and using the sanguine mask

The element of the air lies at the root of the sanguine temperament. Air is always in movement, in and out of our lungs, rising in the heat, sinking in the cold, always responding to external forces. It is the lightest element.

Entering into the imagination of the sanguine element

Following the indications of earth and water, invite the group to imagine a light breeze, with leaves drifting through the air. Invite them to name some of the qualities that they imagine of the air before them, which might include some of these: 'light', 'changeable', 'unpredictable', 'responding to external stimuli'.

Stepping into the image of air, encourage them to feel the lack of resistance, as if the air is within them instead of bones. Encourage them to feel the continually changing nature of air, moving in one direction, the next moment in the other. Let them whip up a bit of chaos by imagining a constantly changing wind, and encourage them rather to submit to the flightiness of the imagination, and to allow their bodily movements, rhythms and gesture to be continually changeable. Their movements will become lighter and more chaotic as the sense of this develops.

Invite them now to walk on the in-breath, to blink the eyes quickly with eyebrows raised in questioning, and enjoy the feeling of being drawn out into the periphery of the body. It is important for the air person that they can feel a joy and buzz in being in the here and now in a continually changing manner; a smile can bring an airy quality, for example difference. The final movement needs to feel natural to the player, not an over-exaggerated, extroverted display of an idea but something that is felt from within.

To conclude, stop the movement, check the feedback regarding how they experience the exercise and find what tendencies individuals might have in common with the rhythmic nature of the airy element, as this could be an indication of their temperament. However, they might find it difficult and tiring.

Experiencing the sanguine body

To help experience the Sanguine through interactive body work, manipulating the limbs is revelatory. Once again it is important to consider the threshold some of these exercises might present, and adjust the experience accordingly. Remind the group of the contract (p 110). Demonstrate the following activity, and supervise subgroups in exploring it for themselves.

The image that accompanies this exercise is of being a puppet manipulated by a number of puppeteers. This exercise is inspired by puppet style from Japan called Bunraku, where the different limbs and head of the puppet are manipulated by different puppeteers. It can be exciting and fun to be the puppet for some but for others it can be quite disturbing, as you don't know when the different parts of your body are going to be moved or why. That's the feeling we need to engender, anyway.

In groups of six, each person takes a turn to be the puppet.

The first person to take a turn stands with space around them in a neutral attitude. The other five take up positions around them, two crouching down by each of the legs, one at each arm and the fifth standing behind them ready to take the head.

One at a time, starting with a leg, one of the manipulators puts a hand around the ankle and slowly squeezes it. When the person being manipulated feels the squeeze they must shift their weight onto the opposite leg and take a small step in the direction that the puppeteer indicates by leading their ankle. The second puppeteer squeezes the second ankle and the procedure is repeated with the second leg taking a step. Having established this, give it a break, and let the arm puppeteers practise their manipulation.

The arm puppeteers take the wrist of the puppet and squeeze it, giving direction to the movement initiated. This can be forward, back, up, down, left to right etc. Having given each arm a practice run, ask them to take a break and introduce the final puppeteer to the head.

Standing behind the puppet, the puppeteer takes hold of the head, one hand at each side, taking care not to cover the ears. Explore simple movements of the head, up down, left to right etc, with clear indications when movement begins and ends. Now, having rehearsed separately, each puppeteer can work at the same time, together in making the puppet walk about and as they become comfortable, go into an eccentric kind of dance. Give the puppet person a number of minutes to really get the feeling of being manipulated. It does not usually take long before they have got the experience and have had enough!

When the first person has finished their experience, invite a second person to take the stand. The person who had been manipulated takes the head, as it will give them a moment to reflect on and absorb the experience before going into activity.

When everyone has had a turn and the exercise is complete, take time for brief feedback. Now invite them to re-create the experience they had without the manipulation from the others. Encourage the group to stand, feeling light and unpredictable, as if they were being manipulated. Now they will be getting into the changeable rhythms and disposition of the Sanguine, and they are ready for the mantra.

The spoken mantra for the Sanguine

With the imagination and body warmed up to the sanguine disposition, introduce the mantra. Try this out and see if it works:

- A mantra for the Sanguine: *'Wow, look at that!'*

With this mantra encourage the group to see specific things of interest in the room and get the others to come over and have a look.

While keeping the bodily gesture they have discovered from the previous exercises, invite the group to say this phrase initially to themselves, then to each other, and after a while, silently to themselves while greeting each other. Now somebody is ready to put on a mask.

Meeting the sanguine half mask

Having approached an individual, remind them to keep doing what they were doing and put the mask on them. As the mask begins to move round the room greeting the others, remind the rest of the group to stop what they are doing and find their way back to neutral.

Be aware of the sanguine energy in the room as the group stops and observes the masked figure. This is usually full of chaos and delight, and unexpected surprise. When the mask has had the opportunity to greet a number of people – this could be running round the room, slapping everyone on the hand – go through the unmasking procedure. Ask the mask wearer to draw themselves up to their full height, close their eyes, taking a breath and go back to neutral. This is time for the feedback:

- What was everyone's experience?
- What new insights do they have about the temperament?

Having debriefed the experience, invite everyone to wash off the airy experience of the Sanguine and bring them back to a more neutral version of themselves.

Preparing and using the choleric mask

The element of fire lies at the root of the choleric temperament. Fire is always hot, burning and consuming fuel, burning up what stands in its path. It is the blood, the heart and ego in the temperament; and it is the most voracious element.

Entering into the imagination of the choleric element

Following the indications of the previous exercises, invite the group to stand in a circle and imagine that before them is a warm fire, with flames licking and consuming the fuel as they glow and burn in the air. Invite them to name some of the qualities inspired by the fire before them: 'Warm', 'hot', 'destructive', 'powerful', 'consuming', 'unpredictable'. Stepping into the imagination of fire, encourage them to feel the strong powerful movement, as if the flames are within them in the place of blood. Encourage them to feel the continually hot and consuming nature of fire, crackling and bursting. Encourage the group to enter into the intensity of the fire person, submitting to the all-consuming quality of this nature, where the movement usually becomes explosive and more frenzied as the idea develops.

Invite them now to work on the sharp in-breath and out-breath and to enjoy the feeling of hot, powerful hunger. It is important for the fire person that they can feel the intensity in going towards the future. The final movement needs to be of a human quality, not over exaggerated, but part of themselves they are able to express naturally through their body.

Stop the movement and check the feedback.

- What did they find familiar to their own tendencies?
- Could this be an indication of their temperament?

Experiencing the choleric body

To help experience the Choleric through interactive body work, offering resistance is revelatory. This exercise might present a challenge, and the appropriate resistance needs to be offered to each person depending on their strength and ability. Demonstrate the following activity with a number of individuals and supervise subgroups to explore it for themselves.

The image that accompanies this exercise is of pushing through others as if in a rugby scrum. This exercise is inspired by gaining ground when strong resistance is encountered. It needs to be exciting and challenging for the pusher; however, care needs to be taken with everyone involved not to overdo it, as with insufficient care, it is possible to strain oneself.

The instruction with this piece is for the pusher to be able to push the scrum a number of paces forward, then to be pushed back a number of paces, and then to break through the group and come out the other side.

In groups of four to six, each person, one at a time, has the opportunity to be resisted.

The first person to take a turn is the pusher; they stand in front of the rest of the group and adopt a neutral attitude. The other five take up positions in front of the pusher in such a way so the pusher can put their head between two people with their arms either side. Another two support the two scrum leaders by standing behind them. There needs to be a final person, who can initially support the feet of the pusher in case they slip. The same person can double as the catcher, who, on the command to part, has moved to stand some way off behind the four scrum members, to catch the pusher when they break through.

A suggested ratio is for the pusher to do five steps forward, the scrum to push them back for four steps, followed by the breakthrough. For the breakthrough, the two scrum members on the right and left will part on a given command – 'Part!' at a point when the pusher is pushing hard. This can be identified by the sound the pusher makes at the optimum moment of resistance. The breakthrough is more of psychological relief than a physical experience, so the catcher is there more as an end marker than a physical catching of the pusher.

When the first person has finished their experience of pushing, invite a second person, one of the scrum, to take the stand. The person who had been pushing might find it helpful to be a back scrum to give them time to catch their breath; it will give them a moment to digest and integrate the experience before going fully into activity.

When everyone has had a turn and the exercise is complete, take time for brief feedback. Was it easy or hard? Was it familiar? Did they enjoy it or not? Now invite them to recreate the experience they had without the resistance of the scrum from the others. While standing, encourage the group to feel the power and force of pushing. Now they will be getting into the future stance of the Choleric, always going forward, and they are ready for the mantra.

The spoken mantra for the Choleric

With the imagination and body warmed up to the choleric disposition, introduce the mantra. Try this out and see if it works:

- A mantra for the choleric: *'This way, follow me!'*

With this mantra, which can serve both for the mature and immature, encourage the individual players to attempt to bring the group to follow their lead. This can be challenging, as there is not enough room for so many leaders and no followers, so do not let it go on for too long.

While keeping the bodily gestures they have discovered from the previous exercises, invite the group to say this phrase initially to themselves, then to each other, and after a while, silently to themselves while greeting each other.

Meeting the choleric half mask

Invite anyone who has embodied this process to put the mask on. As the mask begins to move around the room greeting the others, remind the rest of the group to stop what they are doing and go back to a neutral stance.

Invite the group to notice the choleric energy in the room as the group stops and observes the masked figure. This usually produces a consuming and aggressive ambience, which can be frightening for some. Remind the choleric mask not to get to close to any individual in the room. When the mask has had the opportunity to greet some members of the group, invite them to see if the leader can get the group to follow them out of the door. Clarify for the group that they need only follow if they feel excited by what they might be getting up to with the Choleric, and that they do not need to feel bullied into going along. This is valuable feedback if they do.

Following any exercise, invite the group back into the room and go through the unmasking procedure with the choleric mask: ask them to close their eyes, take a breath, draw up to their full height and go back to neutral, this is time for the feedback.

- What was everyone's experience?
- What new insights do they have about the choleric temperament?

The responses might include remarks about power, adrenalin, fear, creativity, love and anger.

Having debriefed the experience, invite everyone to wash off the fiery experience of the Choleric and bring them back to more neutral version of themselves.

Closure

Having gone through all four of the temperaments, there will be a feeling of familiarity for the group about the nature of the masks. Lay the masks out on the floor, in the order they were introduced, and invite the group to reflect on their experiences of having met each of the temperaments in this way. Invite them to break up into small groups of two or three and reflect together on the following questions:

- What new ideas and information have you encountered through this work?
- What temperaments were you attracted to?
- What temperaments repelled you?
- If you had a dominant temperament, which one do you think it might be?
- What do you think the dominant temperament of your colleagues in the group might be?
- Which temperament feels the most far away from you?

These processes and activities can be a basis for a number of effective developments pushing more deeply into specific fields of practice. In the next chapter I will consider a number of these where the work is taken further into specific subject specialisations.

Chapter 6

MAPS, IMPROVISATIONS, GAMES AND EXERCISES

There are many different exercises, games, improvisations, interactive body work and psychological maps that can be developed from this work, having established a basis for the four temperaments. A number of these are outlined here in this book. However I have heard of different permutations that practitioners have developed with these ideas and practices that have been very effective. The exercise with the strongest emotional impact, from a therapeutic and human developmental point of view, is 'mapping your temperaments', an exercise involving placing masks on the ground around you as a map of how you experience them within you. Another exercise is doing drama improvisations with full masks, in order to see how the different temperaments all approach the same task which is helpful for teachers. Exploring the counter mask is a key for understanding how the temperaments undertake tasks seemingly against character, by overcoming very strong tendencies. Another key exercise is about working with speech and text, colouring it with the temperaments to bring out the nuances of language.

Counter-mask dramas

The counter mask is an idea and practice developed by Jacques Lecoq, which involves bringing more complexity and subtlety to the expression of the mask. This is where we put the extreme mask of a temperament into a situation in which the player has to adapt and develop capacities that are not intrinsically in their nature. In this exercise we will explore how the extreme mask of the temperament needs to be overcome in order to fulfil the task at hand. These situations are the most interesting to watch and participate in, as they reveal the one-sidedness of the dominant nature as well as the potential to be the opposite, which are then poised in conflict with each other. This conflict is a masked drama in itself, and can be deeply revealing and insightful about the temperament and the player.

These pieces can be done in both full and half masks; however, the full mask offers a wealth of understanding through the subtleties of the body language and tempo without needing to go into words.

In the following situations one player is required to be 'charged up' in the mask, while the facilitator, along with a number of volunteers, supports the development of the situation.

The choleric counter-mask drama

Charge the mask up through 'pushing in the rugby scrum' the interactive body work for the Choleric (see p 119), and remind them of the mantra. *'This way, follow me!'* While the mask player is being charged up in another part of the room, brief the group about a simple situation into which the Choleric can enter. When they enter the room in the mask, explain to them the following scenarios.

Scene 1:

The Choleric has lost everything, their relationships have failed, their material goods have been stolen, and the only thing left is to go down upon their knees and pray.

Scene 2:

It is late at night, the baby of the choleric mother or father is crying and can't be stopped. A volunteer makes the crying noises. The mask is invited to come to the aid of the baby. As the mask takes up the baby (a bundle of cloth or a doll) and tries to comfort it, the voice of the crying baby can get qui-

eter, but takes up crying again in a short while, getting louder than before. When the mask wearer seems to be getting the hang of it and the baby is calming down, the baby's pee gets the hands of the wearer wet. He or she then needs to both attend to the needs of the child and the innate nature of the temperament, which is very emphatic and tends toward finding solutions rather than staying with processes.

Watching the Choleric deal with the situation is powerful, as they overcome the tendency of the Choleric to get things sorted and move on, and find the inner calm to attend to the needs of the baby.

The phlegmatic counter-mask drama

Charge up a player in the mask by supporting the feeling of floating (see p 112) and introduce the mantra, *'I like things just the way they are'.* These are good scenarios to use as a starting point.

Scene 1:
The Phlegmatic returns home and finds that all the food has been stolen from the fridge. They have no money and can't contact any friends. The player in the phlegmatic mask needs to explore how, through increasing the tension in the body and developing faster rhythms than the Phlegmatic would normally have, they can develop the emotion of anger. This is a feeling the Phlegmatic would normally avoid.

Scene 2:
Conflict for the Phlegmatic is very difficult and they usually try to avoid it at any cost. This exercise explores how the Phlegmatic might discharge anger. There is a dog on a chair (a cloth bundled up) and a letter that the dog has torn up on the floor. The Phlegmatic is required to give the dog a beating. Initially this is totally ineffective, but gradually the Phlegmatic begins to get into it until it gets carried away and beats the chair rhythmically.

The melancholic counter-mask drama

Charge up a player in the melancholic mask, having them drag somebody along behind and any other aspects of the melancholic interactive body work that the player might need to get into the temperament (see p 108), and invite the player to repeat the mantra, *'No pain no gain.'*

SCENE 1:

The Melancholic enters a dance at a party, and they are encouraged to dance and have fun. The group can sing a song they know for the dance. It is important that the player allows any resistance to doing the dance to be present but overcomes the urge not to dance at all. This can be moving, as it is potentially frivolous, but can be light relief for someone who is normally very serious.

SCENE 2:

There is a pile of costumes, clothes of different colours, hats, jackets shoes etc. The Melancholic is invited to be dressed by two other players who clothe the mask player in outrageous combinations of clothes. The Melancholic is required to allow the dressers to do their job, but not to give over entirely to the experience, setting up the tension between being frivolous and serious at the same time. This can be very funny.

The sanguine counter-mask drama

Charge the player up in the mask with the manipulation exercises or the 'light flicking of the body in the wind' and the mantra, *'Wow, look at this!'* (pp116–117)

SCENE 1:

The Sanguine returns home and everyone, his friends and family, are upset and angry. Try as hard as they like, the Sanguine cannot get them to change their mood. The Sanguine becomes bewildered.

Scene 2:
The Sanguine has lost a dear friend who has died and they go to visit the funeral home and pray.

All the counter-mask dramas can be very moving, as the mask has a fixed state and the action and body image is contrary to the mask's impression. Having explored the counter-mask scenarios, the scope for each temperament mask will have been expanded. This can be a good time to see a number of masks in the same situation.

Temperament crossings

This is the same exercise used for the two neutral masks in Chapter 4. It is called 'crossing in twos', but now with the temperament masks rather than the neutral. This helps in finding both the playfulness and technique of the mask, firstly in relationship to the creative impulse or the player; secondly the relationship between the two masks on the stage and finally the relationship with the audience. By keeping these three relationships alive at any moment, the temperament masks invite us to enter deeply into the relationships between the different temperaments.

Invite two volunteers from the group you are working with to come to the front of the group and put on a full temperament mask of their choice. Have them stand about eight metres apart, or on the opposite sides of the room. Ask them to face the wall, with their backs to each other. When they are calm and focused, invite them to turn round and face each other. Offer them a situation to work in, anything that suggests a tension in the relationship between the masks. The following situations are examples for exploring the temperaments that have come out of a number of workshops:

For Sanguine and Melancholic: *Young adult meets old parent after having not see each other for a number of years.*
Choleric and Melancholic: *Two siblings meet after one has been released from jail.*

PHLEGMATIC AND CHOLERIC: *A couple who have been divided through no choice of their own meet after having not seen each other for a number of years.*
PHLEGMATIC AND SANGUINE: *A woman meets her estranged husband after the success of their child in some enterprise.*

RULES: Mask A looks at the audience, while the B still looks at A. A takes a step toward B while looking at the audience. After this step A looks at B, who takes this as a sign to look out toward the audience. B then looking at the audience takes a step toward A, who is looking at B. This exchange of steps and looks brings A and B very close together for the audience, which has become part of this exchange. When A and B are standing face to face, invite them to resolve the situation by either retracing their steps, or embracing, or walking past each other. Ask them to take off their masks.

In order to learn what worked and what did not, debrief the players after each improvisation, and ask the audience what they saw in relation to the temperaments, the counter mask and the development of the relationship. How did it feel inside the masks? What did they enjoy? What was it like getting closer? Questions for the audience might be: What held their attention? Where were they looking? What did they enjoy?

Full mask dance

As with many pieces of mask improvisation this is something that is also effective with all kinds of masks. In fact I have done this piece with many different masks. However the masks of the temperaments offer the unmasked player more opportunities for understanding and practice in managing extreme types than any masks I have seen. This piece has been created in order to offer an individual the opportunity to experience working with the extreme one-sidedness of the temperaments. Technically this piece is very simple, requiring five volunteers, four to take one of the temperament masks each, and the fifth the role of a dancing or creative movement instructor.

The set up for this is that there is a creative movement class which the four full temperament masks are attending. The unmasked player is the movement tutor whose task it is to engage the four in a creative activity of moving together. This can include stretches, step sequences, movement and imaginative atmospheric instructions for the masks to improvise with.

Ask each of the four volunteers to choose a mask, while an unmasked player helps them charge up the mask by standing in front of the player with the mask on, and pulling a face that resembles the mask in front of them. As the mask performer mirrors back your facial expression, they need to adjust their body to fit with the expression, and so between the masked and the unmasked performer the mask finds its charge. When the masks are charged up, have them prepare for the class before the entrance of the 'tutor'.

The mask players are required to play the mask to the full and not compromise the one-sidedness of the temperament. Explain that the tutor has to get them all to do the same thing, facilitating each of them to achieve the instructions in their own unique way. This can be very funny and challenging, and bring to life the demanding task of working with people who are stuck in one dominant temperament.

A very effective development of this piece could be to suggest that the mask players begin by showing the immature side of the temperament, where they are uncooperative and fixed in their one-sidedness. You can then encourage them to develop into the more mature side of the temperament, where they begin to cooperate with each other, finding their natural place within the sequence and overcoming their one-sidedness with compromising their extreme nature.

This can quite easily culminate with free improvisations during which the strengths and weaknesses of each temperament and their different relationships can become apparent. To conclude, the facilitator needs to bring the class to a close and invite the masks to take a bow. Following the bow, the masked performers need to turn away from the audience, pull themselves up to their full height, and take the masks off.

Mapping the temperaments

This process has been developed from the idea that the temperament lies between the soul and body, as a psychology that interfaces between the two. The soul uses the temperaments to work through the senses and the body's portal for the physical experience to enter into consciousness. The temperament is an interface that enables the perceptions to be conceptualised, both through the vehicle of the constitution brought over from heredity and also that which we bring with us as our eternal core from before birth.

The mapping process can be done in twos or threes, with each person having a chance to be the mapper supported by the other two.

Ask each group to place a chair in the centre of a demarcated space in which the composition of the temperament map can be developed – a large carpet can work well. By laying the masks of the temperaments out on the floor around us, we can describe how we experience each temperament within our lives. The mapper sits on the chair with the four masks of the temperaments out in front of them about 3 metres in front. The mapper asks a supporter to take a mask and place it in a location somewhere around the chair.

If a participant sitter places a mask in front of the chair this tends to indicate that this temperament has a leading role in the life of the sitter. The mask in front also suggests that the sitter is conscious of it. If the mask is facing forward it could suggest the temperament is facing the world, and if it's facing back, possibly that the temperament is in conflict to the sitter who might be looking to develop it.

If it's placed behind the mapper it usually indicates the temperament or temperaments that are more distant or unconscious. It could be that the sitter is unaware of them or that they are over aware of the power of this temperament and are hiding from it in some way. This could be due to childhood events or trauma.

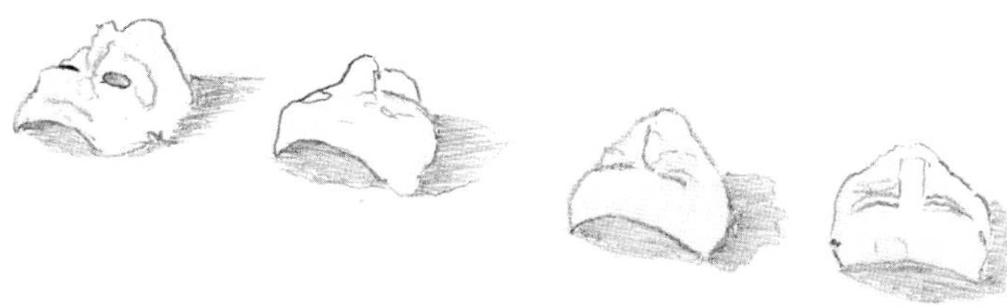

To the left or right can have meaning too: on the left of the sitter suggests the more rational and cognitive part of the brain. The right usually indicates the more intuitive sense of the temperament. This is the feeling side, where there is more creativity and spontaneous sensing for life. This can however also be determined by the mapper and interpreted in whatever way feels relevant to them.

This piece of work need to be undertaken quite quickly and spontaneously, so as not to do it by numbers or logic, but more by a intuitive feeling process. Sometimes mappers ask for a mask to be placed upside down, under a cloth, or outside of the frame. On a number of occasions mappers have put a mask on the chair. This might indicate a very dominant temperament or a pride or fear of a dominant temperament.

The complexity of the sitter's choice is a very personal experience, and it is not helpful in this work to question why the choices have been made. Rather, what is helpful is to offer the sitter the opportunity to change the map if they could.

When all four of the masks have been placed around the chair, invite the mapper to stand up and come over to the front and look at the chair with the masks around it. Seeing the image from the outside can be very revealing for the mapper. This might be a time when the mapper shifts a mask for clarification. What can be helpful at this point is to put the neutral mask on the chair, indicating that there is a deep inner part of the person that is not associated with the temperaments, but is independent of them. To further this experience, the mapper can choose one of the supporters to sit in the chair with the neutral mask on and imagine that it is they who are sitting there. This gives an experience of seeing oneself from the outside, offering an objective perspective.

This is the chance to ask the mapper the key question: if they could move one mask to a different position in their map, which mask would they move, and where would they move it to?

The mapper can indicate this by moving the mask. Invite the mapper to sit once again in the order to see how it feels with the mask moved to a different position. This can be left as an indication of how they might like to develop themselves in the future. Asking them how they might undertake an activity in their lives in the future to support making this adjustment in their map, they can commit to developing some self care and development in the future.

Following this experience the mapper can find it useful to do a small drawing of the map, indicating the move they would like to make. I will consider how this process can be used in different contexts in the next chapter.

Temperament masks in speech and communication development

You will need the four half temperament masks and a neutral, a table and a mirror.

This piece is really about performing in front of others, in order to develop temperaments that feel difficult to access and understand. This can also mean developing performance techniques if the group is performance orientated. I will consider this application in the next chapter on using the temperament masks in different contexts.

Whatever the emphasis of the group, it is important that the work offers the participants fun, support and creative solutions to the subtle problems of communication. No one is right or wrong – everyone is different and we all have work to do in realising more potential in our lives and work.

Speech development in different temperaments

Invite individuals to think of a short piece of text they can use in the masks. Something they know off by heart, a song, nursery thyme, poem or speech from a play, for example. Once they have chosen something, get them to walk the text, one syllable at a time on each step to break any habitual way of speaking the lines. Now invite them to walk around in pairs, and one at a time to talk the text to their partner. The partner can ask questions for clarification. Remind them not to slip into the predetermined rhythm of the chosen text or the way they are used to speaking it.

Each person in the couple now has the chance to deliver the text in four different ways: firstly while pushing their partner, then by dragging their partner, then by being supported by their partner, and finally by being 'manipulated like a puppet' by their partner. Demonstrate light, playful ways of doing this using the different approaches to access the temperaments and using interactive body work and mantras. Let each person take it in turn to present their text in each of the temperaments.

Animating the masks with speech and movement

Set up a table with a mounted mirror on it. Place all four of the half temperament masks on the table in front of the mirror, the neutral masks among them. The mirror should face the audience, so if the player is looking in the mirror their back is to the audience. Set up the audience about 4–5 metres from the performance space, placing a defining line between the performance space and the audience, which the masks are not allowed to go over. This can be done using a rope or cloth.

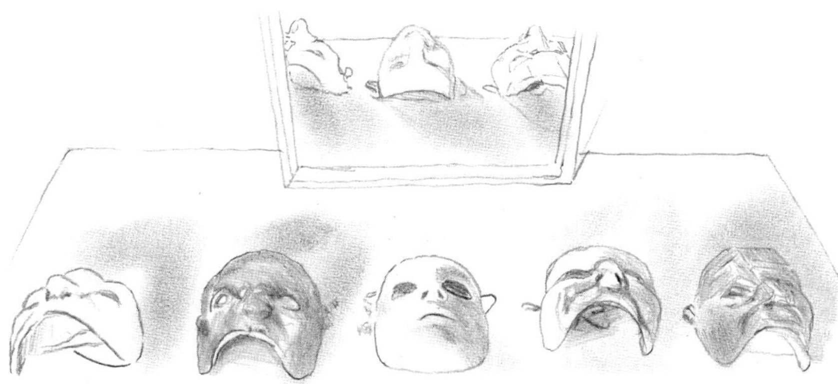

Ask each player, one at a time, to stand in front of the audience with their back to them, facing the table. Ask them to put on the neutral mask, look at themselves and try to get back into a neutral stance, letting go of any tension or planning any performance ideas. Now ask them to spontaneously choose any of the four masks they feel drawn to. This could be the one that they feel most confident about or the one that jumps out at them when you look at all four. Ask them to put it on, look in the mirror and encourage the player to find the breath and body architecture that fits the mask. After a few seconds, for that is all they have, ask them to turn around and face the audience. They should look at the audience directly, making eye contact, the chosen temperament bubbling inside the mask. Now ask them to start delivering the chosen text in the manner of the given temperament mask.

Once they have gone through the text, speaking it to the audience in the manner of the mask, ask them to turn around and walk back to the table. They should then take the mask off, breathe, and come back to themselves.To do this they should put the neutral mask back on to help let go of the previous mask.

Choose the next mask and continue through these stages. Eye contact is essential in this work otherwise the audience will lose interest in what you're doing and not hear what you're saying.

Go through each of the four masks, delivering the text in different ways highlighted by the temperament you are investigating. Here are some YouTube clips of improvised speech that might be useful:

SANGUINE: https://www.youtube.com/watch?v=KzonbL5IPxY
CHOLERIC: https://www.youtube.com/watch?v=E_eBGGHWBhs
MELANCHOLIC: https://www.youtube.com/watch?v=duK2c0qIWac
PHLEGMATIC: https://www.youtube.com/watch?v=5E7niWOPBnE

It is important to let the players know this is optional, while encouraging them to have a go; it's also important to make it clear there is no right or wrong, only differences.

When the first person has completed their round of speaking in all four of the half-temperament masks, the following interaction can support the development of the temperament that the player struggled with the most. One temperament is always weaker. Ask them which one they think it is, and see if the group agrees. Whichever one it is, offer them the opportunity to try it again with the relevant support. Here are some ideas on how the group might do that.

If the Sanguine is the weaker temperament

Support them by manipulating their limbs in the same way suggested in the previous chapter (p 116), while they have the mask on and are speaking their text. Encourage them to let go and allow the text to be influenced by the involuntary movements of the puppeteers.

This inevitably frees the player up, as they can't control what they are doing in quite the same manner.

If the Phlegmatic is the weaker temperament

Invite the player to sit on a chair, or stand, while a group of five around them takes the weight of their arms, and if sitting, legs as well. Ask the group to move them rhythmically and calmly in circles. Encourage them to allow the floating feeling to inform the text and bring in a calm, soft feeling.

This usually relaxes the speech and communication style, and if the speaker is sitting, invite them to stand and keep the feeling of support without the others taking the weight of their limbs.

If the Choleric is the weaker temperament

If the Choleric has been identified, keep the protagonist in the mask and build up a rugby scrum in front of them, made up of two to four supporters. Ask the player to communicate their text while trying to break through to the audience. The protagonist needs to be offered resistance in order to meet the fire and power within them to go beyond the resistance and communicate with the audience.

This can be quite exhilarating for some people and it can also be a huge surprise to find the power they can harness.

If the Melancholic is the weaker temperament

Offer the protagonist the 'shopping bags,' made up of one or two supporters sitting behind them holding their wrists, while the speaker walks forward dragging them. Remind them that they have to resign to the weight and not fight it. What can be helpful here is the resistance at the back of the head, weighing it down, and the resistance from behind holding the ankles, like a ball and chain.

With all of this work, make sure to offer them plenty of support and praise for any incremental steps that might have been taken in accessing temperaments that are often far out of reach.

These supports and resistances can shift the speaker from their default temperament, and bring them into the under-developed temperament. If you have other ideas that arise spontaneously to create physical supports and resistances, you might develop something more appropriately based on the needs of the individual speakers you are working with. For example, on one occasion an entire group picked up the protagonist and slowly rocked them, which gave them the relaxation they needed in order to be really convincing with their Phlegmatic aspect.

On another occasion, the player working on developing the Sanguine was supported by having four people out front giving them different instructions that interfered with what they were planning to do. They had to copy the arm movements of one person, while doing the steps of another; they were also asked the answer to simple arithmetic and gave the answers to the question quietly, while continuing with the text. This was great fun for the speaker and all involved.

We have looked at the four temperaments, meeting them in their natural environment, pushing them to see how to manage them and where their thresholds are, when the cracks appear and how different approaches can be useful. We have looked at suggestions of supporting the development of different temperaments in order to ameliorate over-developed temperaments, and how to strengthen under-developed ones. In the next chapter I will explore in what situations and contexts this work can be applied.

Chapter 7

APPLICATIONS OF TEMPERAMENT MASKS IN DIFFERENT CONTEXTS

There are many areas of life and a number of fields of practice that I have applied aspects of this work: as a parent, as a psychotherapist in the therapeutic arena, in training actors for the stage, in the context of social renewal and teacher training, and contributing to the fields of corporate development and medicine. I will consider briefly how I have used this work in my own practice, but also how I have supported others in the fields of their own work and practice.

Therapeutic applications

I have used a number of these ideas and practices in my therapeutic practice with young adults with complex needs. A number of counsellors and therapists have described how effective the masks can be in supporting a therapeutic process with clients. For those who work in the field of counselling, therapy, psychodrama, dramatherapy and so on, the following applications may bring insight and relief to clients. I have used these masks, exercises and processes in two specific ways.

Masks of temperaments as emotional states

In my practice I have invited clients to use the masks in ways described in the mapping exercise (see pp 130–132). With young adults going through puberty and the threshold of adolescence, the masks can be used to identify emotions and feelings that the clients might be experiencing. This can be a very significant intervention for people who struggle with language and the verbalisation of what they're experiencing. Often such clients have been able to use the masks as indications of emotions that they feel. Even though the temperaments are not emotions in themselves, each of them in the extreme can give rise to associated emotional states.

As we will see in the work with the self development of teachers, the unbridled temperament can become emotionally overbearing: the Choleric can push into anger, the Melancholic into sadness, the Sanguine into playful chaos and the Phlegmatic into boredom. By using the masks as indications of these feelings and emotions, the client can describe how they feel each of these emotions in the present time. Through mapping feelings, the client can begin to remember and articulate what caused such feelings. By asking what feelings they would ideally like to be experiencing, and mapping those, the distance between how they feel, and how they would like to feel becomes visible. They can then explore how to get from the one state to the other.

Over-dominant temperament as an indication of trauma

Taking the previous exercise a step further, if the client has the ego strength to go into such an intervention, it can be helpful for the client to look at over-dominant temperaments as an indication of trauma. This is where the psychotherapeutic work comes in, and the psychodramatic action methods can be very supportive in this regard.

What can follow in deepening the client work is finding the moments in biography that have given rise to a stuck or overbearing temperament. This could be considered as learned behaviours that defend the self (or if you prefer, the ego) from being threatened by trauma; here explore how one might work with the masks in that context. The mask can become representative of a person in the client's history, someone who has made a significant impact on the client's beliefs, behaviour and emotional state. This can

often be the perpetrator of an act of abuse. With the container of the mask, often used as a symbol, the client can express the affect that might need a voice, and begin a process of developmental repair. The mask can be a very useful tool in being able to address parts of the self. I use masks regularly in my work in a forensic, democratic therapeutic community with men who have been abused. The mask often represents that part of them that has been neglected and abused, and they can now, as an adult, begin to take care of that part of themselves symbolically in the mask.

It has been proven as an effective tool in developing emotional intelligence, relieving stress arising from emotional states and exploring origins of emotional states.

Application in schools and teacher training

Both the mask-making and using techniques as well as the processes described in this book have been used with pupils in schools and for teacher training. In mask making there are a number of applications for different ages and projects.

Mask making for pupils in schools

There are three areas that have been particularly effective in teacher training, both for comprehensive teachers attending inset training workshops and for Steiner Waldorf teachers. The first is in regard to mask making, as the techniques indicated in this book are easily applicable for craft teachers and in set building for the stage.

Mask making for younger pupils can be best used to enter into the mythology that the pupils might be studying. For example, the Norse mythology for the younger classes for pupils around nine to ten years old, and Greek for eleven to twelve year olds. The same method is applied in making the mask.

The theme of the temperaments is interesting for older pupils from twelve years to fourteen. Here the approach indicated works very well as the onset of the adolescence approaches with the inner awakening of deep feelings, where the psychology of the temperaments can be of interest. The experience that the power of feelings and emotions can be felt more strongly by each of the different temperaments can help with the insight that this is part of natural development. The Choleric can feel righteous anger toward wrongs they perceive; the Melancholic can feel the sadness for the suffering of the world; the Sanguine can experience the manic highs and brief lows in response to meeting life's challenges; and the Phlegmatic has the tendency to go inward and not participate in the extremes of feeling that might confront the other temperaments.

For older pupils making masks for the plays they are doing – from Shakespeare to *commedia dell'arte*, the same techniques can be very effectively used.

Mask using in schools

I have only taught in schools using the temperament masks on a small number of occasions; however a large number of English and drama teachers have used my masks of the temperaments over the years and shared their experiences and applications.

Maths

In Steiner schools the four 'gnomes' of addition, subtraction, multiplication and division are well associated with the four temperaments. Addition is associated with the red Choleric as it is adding up as if going forward, subtraction is associated with the blue melancholic temperament as it is taking away as if going backwards; multiplication connects to the yellow Sanguine, leaping forward in big bounding steps; and division with the green Phlegmatic, calmly fitting parts into one and other. A number of teachers have used the temperament masks to embody the four functions and play a sketch of each of their functions.

English

The process and exercises of developing speech of the temperaments (pp 88–90) is very effective with fourteen to sixteen year olds who are working with poems and on presentation skills. In the application of the temperament speech exercise where the participant is asked to 'colour' a piece of text, the temperaments can be introduced through the blind mask exercises. This can prepare the way for text work through the mantras and then into choosing a small piece of text, a poem, song or rhyme. By repeating the same piece in each of the different temperament half masks, they can be encouraged to express themselves more fully through the interactive body work (see Chapter 5), which can help them to explore and experience their range of feelings and the mastery they can develop over them.

Speech

As in the approach above, the same piece of text can be replaced by the four speech exercises. Here they are below.

- Melancholic: *'Moisten mason mine essence.'*
- Choleric: *'Come crooked craftiest cur.'*
- Phlegmatic: *'By beaten bowers bide brave.'*
- Sanguine: *'Lovely lady leading lipping light laughter.'*

Go through the general speech exercises first, after which the voice will be warmed up for mask work. Now in each of the masks practise the speech exercise strongly in each of the temperaments. This will help the player accentuate the speech work and bring colour and articulation to their speaking.

Improvising

An effective development, having introduced the temperaments through speech, is to give free reign for the potential for play and improvisation that the masks seem to be so good at creating.

The first rich area for improvising is with the full masks. Explore the counter-mask for each of the temperaments, looking at how each one can find a broader range of expression. The exploration of the four full masks attending a dance class (pp 129–130) gives rich improvisation scope for the class. Park bench improvisations are also very effective in full temperament masks: set up a situation where a mask meets another on a park bench. For example, one mask fancies the other while the second is very shy. The crossing exercise is very good for improvisation exploring the encounter of the different combinations of temperaments in pairs (p 127).

In half masks the improvisation of singing a song in the extremes of the temperaments involves letting go, working as a group and exploring the extremes of the temperaments. Taking a song that the class knows, invite four of them to put a mask of each of the temperaments on, and have them find a way of singing the song without compromising the temperament, but still singing in tune.

Drama

Having explored the full masks crossing in twos and meeting in the middle, introduce a third mask. Coming on from one of the sides, the two in the middle face the new one, and the two do the crossing together at the same time alternating with the first one to meet in the middle. It is important to keep the three different focuses going: with one's inner spontaneity, the other masks on the stage, and the audience. This can be rehearsed and repeated, cutting out the excessive looks at the audience, and breaking convention for effect. Give the masks a context, suggesting that the one is the mother, meeting the daughter who she has not seen for ten years. Then the old boyfriend of the daughter comes on and meets the two of them. In this way you can build up a narrative of relationships that can be rehearsed and performed.

This final piece is very useful as a preparation for pupils in early adolescence as a preparation for *commedia dell'arte*.

Teacher training

A number of these processes and exercises are very useful for teachers to get to know their temperaments, and to consider how best to ameliorate some of their own tendencies which might be overbearing when it comes to working with pupils.

The question with teacher training and the four temperaments is primarily, 'What we should do as a teacher to subdue or even to take in hand to educate our own temperament can only be answered if we pursue the basic matter of what effect the teacher's temperament has on the children simply through the fact of it being there.' (Steiner, 2009)

Overbearing choleric teacher

If the choleric teacher expresses themselves in violent ways and the children are frightened, the child may feel afraid in the presence of that teacher all the time and end up feeling miserable. Steiner suggests that this can affect the person in adulthood. If the teacher does not practise self-education with children as young as eight or nine, this can recur in adulthood so that around the age of forty-five or fifty the person can develop metabolic illnesses. These illnesses can manifest in weak digestion, gout and even psychological conditions of anxiety.

What is important for the choleric teacher in their self-education is learning the ability to suppress their violent nature and hold it in check. This is a quality helped immensely by the exercises with masks arising from mapping the temperaments around themselves (pp 130–132), identifying the Choleric, going into the interactive bodywork of pushing and learning to restrain themselves.

To counteract this overbearing tendency, let them be on the receiving end of the pushing structure to see the power it takes to hold back that potentially violent energy (p 85). This could involve using aspects of the therapeutic work in going back into their biography to see where their choleric temperament became violent before and using that as a measuring tool for managing and controlling their temperamental force. This might go further back into trauma of some kind.

Overbearing phlegmatic teacher

If a teacher has an over-developed phlegmatic temperament and expresses themselves as if they don't really care, the pupils can become impulsive and psychologically breathless. The child who wants to get going may then feel an inner impulsiveness wanting to come out, which can lead to feelings of nervousness. Steiner suggests that the affect this can have for the person in adulthood is a disorganisation of the nervous system leading to nervousness and neurasthenia, a chronic fatigue, at the ages of forty-five to fifty.

What is very helpful for the phlegmatic teacher in their self-education is learning the ability to bring in a playfulness and vigour to their work, and not just stick to the facts.

To help develop this, again the mapping exercise is very useful (pp 130–132); when they identify their dominant phlegmatic temperament, enable the interactive bodywork (pp 116–117) for the Sanguine. This is the temperament of childhood. If they are on the giving and receiving end of the manipulation structure they will experience the changeability and spontaneity that children need. As with the Choleric, this could involve using aspects of the therapeutic work in going back into their biography to see where their phlegmatic temperament became excessively indolent and using that as a measuring tool for going beyond themselves and controlling their temperamental lethargy.

Overbearing melancholic teacher

In the case of the over-developed melancholic teacher who might be preoccupied with themselves, they may lose touch with the children in the class. This can lead the children to hide their feelings in the presence of that teacher all the time and end up feeling unmet. Steiner suggests that this can affect the person in adulthood if the teacher does not practise self-education with children so that around the age of forty-five or fifty the pupil can develop irregular blood circulation, which can lead to heart disease.

What is important for the melancholic teacher in their self-education is learning the ability to come out of their self-absorption through rising to the interest of their pupils and going beyond themselves. They need to fire their interest into the future. This is a quality helped by the exercises with masks arising from mapping the temperaments (pp 130–132), identifying the Melancholic, going into the interactive body work of dragging and learning (pp 108–109) to consciously lighten their load. Let them be

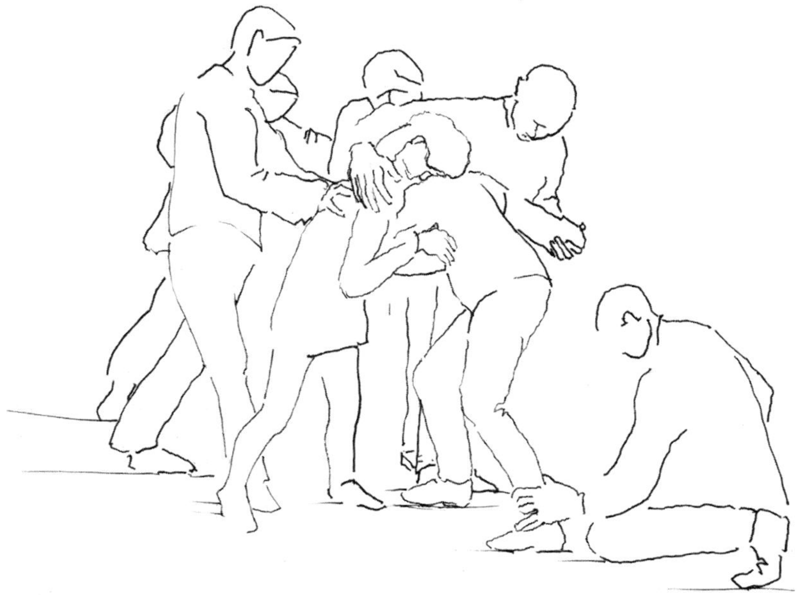

in the dragging end of the structure to see the pain it takes to hold that 'preoccupied' energy. It is also helpful for the Melancholic to experience the choleric interactive body work, to find the interest that the child needs, for the future. This could involve using aspects of the therapeutic work, looking at where their melancholic temperament became most preoccupied, and using that as a measuring tool for managing and controlling their temperamental preoccupation.

Overbearing sanguine teacher

If the over-developed sanguine teacher expresses themselves only through fleeting interactions and makes no deep impression, the children may feel a lack of vitality and they lose their 'strength of will'. (Steiner, 2009) Steiner suggests that this can affect the person in adulthood, giving rise to the pupil developing a pathological lack of zest for life later on.

What is important for the sanguine teacher in their self-education is learning the ability to fight against their tendency to move on and hold their attention on one deep subject. This is really helped by using the exercises of mapping (pp 130–132), identifying the sanguine temperament, and going into the interactive bodywork (pp 116–117). Being on the receiving end of this can reveal how tiring it can be to be compelled to change continually. Once again this could involve using aspects of the therapeutic work looking at where their sanguine temperament became predominantly superficial in the teacher's biography and using that as a measuring tool for managing and controlling their temperamental short span of attention.

In order to consider how trauma might have impacted on the over-development of a temperament, working with a qualified therapist using the masks might be an effective route for exploration.

Organisational development and developing leaders

A number of the practices in this book have been used very effectively in training managers and leaders in developing their presentation skills. A popular application is the structure in which each mask presents a piece of spoken text (pp 132–137).

This is prepared by doing the four pieces of interactive bodywork developed for each of the four temperaments: pushing for the Choleric; floating for the Phlegmatic; manipulating for the Sanguine and dragging for the Melancholic. Having established the nature and dynamics of each of the four temperaments, the participants are invited to choose a particular theme to present to the rest of the group, something

Choleric bodywork

Phlegmatic bodywork

Sanguine bodywork

Melancholic bodywork

no longer than two minutes. With the structure set up with the four half masks and the neutral as a reference to find the calm centre, invite them to present in each of the four half-temperament masks, bringing the presentation alive in the manner of each temperament.

As in the previous exercise follow the procedure of supporting the presenter in developing the temperament that is weakest or perhaps the one most challenging. Now take the masks away from the presenter and give them to the rest of the group watching. Invite them to put the masks on, in order to be an 'extreme temperament audience', which can offer the most challenges for the presenter to engage with.

The presenter is now unmasked, but has to play to the members of the audience in the manner of the temperament they are looking at. Get them to connect to each of the temperaments during the presentation, finding moments in their presentation that might engage one temperament and then change to deliver another manner in the presentation to another temperament. In this way they move their focus round to include each of the different temperaments of audience members, in a training exercise designed to keep an audience, with their different temperaments engaged.

This can, at first, be strong and extreme and when the presenter gets the hang of changing, they can make it less extreme if necessary, and find a natural level that keeps each temperament engaged from time to time. I have used this piece in working with classes at the Cranfield School of Management in presentation training workshops.

Staff development

During away days and inset training a number of these exercises and processes have been very effectively used by a number of practitioners. The use of masks to elucidate the psychology of the four temperaments can shed light on relating to all client bases.

Here are two practices that have been used with large groups. I have used the following activities in the Ruskin Mill Trust to help staff bond, develop trust, have some common insights about the client base they are working with, and have some fun together.

Blind masks

Use the exercise of blind masks (pp 106–107), where a volunteer is invited to stand before the group with their eyes closed. One of the four temperament masks is put on their face. Starting in a neutral stance, without any conscious attitude, the volunteer looks out through the eyes of the mask at the rest of the group looking back at them. The inner question they ask is, 'Who am I?' Ask the different members of the group take up postures, gestures and attitudes that they feel the mask should have to make it congruent, and give the volunteer more of a sense of who they are. When each of the masks have been met through the blind encounter, all four can be seen up in front at the same time.

Ask the members of the group:

- What did you feel were familiar personal traits?
- Could you identify clients, colleagues and students you work with?
- Do you feel changed by any of the temperaments and why?

Questions for small group reflection could include:

- What new ideas and information have you encountered through this work?
- What temperaments were you attracted to?
- What temperaments repelled you?
- If you had a dominant temperament, which one do you think it might be?
- What do you think the dominant temperament of your colleagues in the group might be?
- Which temperament feels the most far away from you?

This piece can be developed further by asking the small groups to reflect on how they might get the best out of each temperament. This can be insightful if they think about what temperaments might dominate in the constitution of various clients they are working with, and what might help in managing them in the most effective way.

For someone working in an organisation, dealing with clients or pupils, or developing leaders who line manage others, these processes can be very effective. A study of the temperaments can give good indication on levels of pitching when approaching staff, so they can feel really seen and met in order to get the best out of them. In order to experience each of the temperaments role play is very effective. Below are a number of scenarios that can help staff with clients, and leaders with staff they are line managing. Engaging with the temperament of clients, pupils or staff is what is required.

However it requires astute observation to get the measure of the temperaments of those you encounter. The most effective exercise for this is speaking to an audience in 'Temperament masks in speech and communication development' because the player in the mask will find the temperament closest to themselves easiest to play (on p 132).

Here you have to have prepare yourself beforehand by going through each of the four half masks, and accessing the energy of the temperament. Invite each participant to choose something they have to say to another colleague. Get them to practise it in pairs in each of the four temperaments, and then swap around to give the other in the pair a chance to do it.

This might feel like a lot of work; however when this becomes second nature, the work is done intuitively and very quickly and you will get a sense of what temperament each individual could be.

It is good to remember with the exercise that: the Choleric loves passion and a call to adventure; the Melancholic the deep, painful and significant moments in life; the Sanguine playful humour and the unexpected; and the Phlegmatic the calm balanced and rhythmic aspects of life.

The use of masks for actors

Masks have been developed in training actors predominantly through the work of Jacques Lecoq. In his school in Paris, Lecoq used different mask styles to develop different qualities, capacities and skills in his students. From the neutral, the naive, *commedia dell'arte* and the clown, the mask focused on the present here and now moment, playing spontaneously with what presents itself, and keeping the relationship to the audience and the other masks on the stage in mind all the time.

Actor training

All the exercises in this book are very effective in training actors for the stage. From the early work of introducing the four elements, the actor can develop an atmosphere for their characters. In the same way as the interactive body work has been suggested, the physical muscle memory of the characters that the actor is required to play can be a key for getting in touch with the physicality of the character. The mantra that has been developed for each of the temperaments (pp 109–121 *passim*) is the next key for the actor working on the development of their characters throughout the duration of the play. A mantra, the inner unconscious statement of intent, exists for any character in a play, if you can find it; and it can change during the development of the play. At one point, for example, the character might be saying to themselves: 'Wake up, follow me!' and after a significant moment in the play this could change to: 'I like things just the way they are.'

The four temperament masks can also be used for colouring the text (pp 133–137), as we have seen. In a drama college where I taught for ten years I used the same piece to help them colour the text in a different spontaneous manner. What worked best was when I held the masks and used them as indications of what temperament to speak out of; this gave the actors an experience of a rich colouring of the text that they had not considered. They could then take this to enrich the speech. Actors have found it useful to use highlight markers in the colours of the four temperaments to mark their text with. By colouring specific words and sentences with a specific colour it helps to give feeling and energy to the speeches.

This book is not the place to go into the rich and effective field of the role of masks in actor training other than to say the mask's role is to enliven and discipline actors, increasing the dynamic and creative approach to acting.

Social renewal and community development

The full programme of the work described in this book has been used in different ways in social therapeutic centres to support community development, social renewal and staff training. The processes of using masks in conjunction with the psychology of the four temperaments can offer not only personal and educational insights, but social interaction that can deepen the understanding of relationships. Living in a Camphill community, for example (social therapeutic centres for people with complex needs), offers an aesthetic and holistic environment. With often exciting projects and seasonal activities and the rich supportive relationships between co-workers and villagers, these environments seem ideal. However, this can also present challenges that need to be dealt with if they are not to take over the positive aspects of community living in a Camphill-type setting. Unspoken tensions from fear to resentment, misunderstanding and failed idealism can splinter communities. However Rudolf Steiner suggests that living in community has the potential for individuals to awaken to each other through encounter, and '... to wake up in the encounter with the soul and spirit of his fellow man. He wants to awaken to his soul and spirit, to approach him in a way that startles his soul and spirit awake in the same sense that light and sound and other such environmental elements startle one out of dreaming.' (Steiner, 1994)

The process by which human beings can awaken each other through encounter can be enabled by many of the exercises in this book, particularly mapping the temperaments, which gives participants insights and empathy into the psychology of each other. Through considering others in how the temperaments live within you begins the process of developing more trust, tolerance and empathy with those around. By sharing with each other we begin to soften and let each other into our feelings, and we also begin to understand what make others tick. This process can have a transformative affect on community life, enabling a culture of learning, sharing and support of individuals within community.

When living and working in community we need to get to know each other, which playful artistic exchange can engender. Like in a marriage, if we know that someone is struggling with something, we can be more tolerant, especially if they are in some manner asking for help. It must always be remembered that this is 'holy' work, as we are required to be open and sensitive and available for the reflection and feedback from others.

Chapter 8

STORIES FROM PRACTICE

Having worked with masks for over thirty years there have been many moments in performances and workshops in both making and using masks where I've seen some incredibly moving and inspiring scenes and conversations. These easily compare with theatrical productions and films I have seen. What follows are some examples of mask making and using with the neutral and the four temperaments, which speak of the transformative nature of mask in the role of identity.

No melancholics in Wellingborough Prison

In 1998 I was invited to do a day's workshop in a high-security prison with lifers. I went in armed with masks of the four temperaments and neutral masks. Beginning with the neutral, I introduced the concept that the mask embodies no past or future, not age or youth, it is neither male nor female, happy or sad It is potentially all of these things. The guys were right up to all the work. They had done various drama workshops before and did not hold back. The neutral mask work was far more authentic and focused than any drama student I had taught in the three drama colleges I had worked at. We did the Lecoq piece of waking up for the first time, with no past or future.

In this exercise the group is invited to lie down and close their eyes as if they are asleep. They are asked not to have any thoughts about the past or future but to keep their attention firmly focused on the present, the things they can see, feel, touch and hear. Then they are invited to stand up slowly as if for the first time, and encounter their own body, the floor, each other and the audience.

The work was astounding, as if through the mask they were escaping from the bounds of prison and moving into a freedom beyond their crime and biographical impediments.

This was followed by work with the Choleric, which they immediately mastered, tapping into all their anger and testosterone. The Sanguine became a trickster joker, flighty and hilarious. The Phlegmatic was calm and cool beyond measure. The Melancholic however never got a look in. Not one of the men would try it on. It would have led them into a place of sadness, loneliness and loss that they were not in a position to allow themselves to go into. The danger of crying and feeling the pain would have got them into more trouble than it was worth. The astounding work they had done with the Neutral and the resistance to the Melancholic was not my experience when working in a therapeutic prison, but really understandable for the conditions of a mainstream prison.

Being fully in the present

At a drama college in London I taught mask work and physical theatre for over a ten-year period. As with performances in workshops and training sessions, those profound moments can slip under the radar of great theatre, and this would have been most definitely one, had the circumstances not asked for an addendum. A class of second-year students were doing neutral mask; we had been doing it for some months, creating a basis for neutral action by stripping away all the painful idiosyncrasies that can go unnoticed. The exercise required that the masked performer wake up as if for the first time, look out upon a seascape and wave goodbye to a friend, then turn and run away. Time upon time we failed, bringing in emotions and stories to the exercise that become a distraction from the focus. We were tired, it was the end of the day, when Mandy, a giggling eighteen-year-old, agreed to give it a last try. We all watched without expectation. You know that feeling, when you are in a group of people, and slowly everyone goes quiet, the inner and outer chatter stops and you hold your breath as if you don't want to disturb the magic. Presence is profound, it is pure grace, and Mandy could have done anything, her body and actions did not indicate any previous experience, enabling the audience to enter into her action as if the audience was her. Afterwards, there was a slow clap that broke to a roar. 'What part did you enjoy the most?' I asked, 'How was it for you?'

'I don't know,' Mandy said, 'I can't remember anything.' This is what I would posit as moving into the realm of the here and now. It is that place where action becomes selfless, and yet so full of a bigger self, that the audience feels they are the ones who have been moving.

Robbing banks

I was working with a company doing artistic work with ex-cons on probation, to support their transition back into the outside world. I was working with the four temperaments and the neutral mask, which all went well until discussion at the end when I had a challenging realisation about different uses of masks. There were twelve men, all over the age of thirty, the oldest being John at sixty-four. We were having tea after the session, when John come up and told me he had used masks many times when he was younger. I was happily surprised, and asked him what kind. He said had he been an actor and that he had been very successful in using them; that they had worked very well. 'What theatre were you in?' I asked. 'I used them as a disguise to rob banks.' Quite shocked, I asked him how he had found working with the masks in a theatre/personal development context. He said it was more scary, as he did not know what to do and he did not have a gun. It goes to show how versatile masks can be.

Making my demon self

Running a workshop on making a mask based on the four temperaments, a young woman studying drama therapy said she wanted to make a choleric mask. As she began forming the face, the design took on a number of phases. Firstly it was strong and muscular, like a super hero with strong chin and determined eyebrows. Then it became more old and decrepit, like the angry witch Babayaga determined to destroy Vasilisa the Beautiful from the Russian folk tale. The third phase found a combination of the two that remained through to painting. On enquiring about what the mask might mean for the young woman, she said, 'This is a part of me that I am in a dire battle with. Sometimes it consumes me, at other times it helps me. I am determined to become its master, for it has become too destructive.'

The therapeutic use of mask work can be a useful process for gaining insight about some of our feelings, beliefs and behaviours. The mask has a fixed image, which in itself does not move, although it might appear to in different movements and in changes of light. The fixed nature of the mask enables the user to explore the fixed, one-sidedness that the mask portrays. By getting to know some of these dimensions we might have, something Jung might call the shadow, or Steiner the double, we learn to anticipate their effect on us, and become more able to choose the behaviour we exhibit, rather than be overcome by it.

Some months later we met in town, and I asked how her mask work was getting on. She said with a smile: 'Very good thanks, we are on much better terms now.' I think she is very courageous, because sometimes it seems that by going into the darkness we can find the light.

Closing thoughts

In working on the inside and outside of the mask, a relationship begins to develop between what is seen and what is still unseen. What the mask maker leaves out allows room for the imagination and more space for the player to inhabit. If the mask has too much information, the player would have to be so still so as not to become a blur; the mask had rather be a sculpture for the audience to walk around at their own leisure. The psychology of masks as they challenge the notion of identity invites us to reconsider who the 'self' or the 'other' might be. The elemental psychology of the temperaments seems to awaken an ancient tacit knowledge of human nature, inviting us to consider the masks we might be wearing. These masks are not cultural, or social, but rather correspond to a constitutional self situated somewhere between the body and the soul.

Bibliography

Brook, Peter. *There Are No Secrets*, 1993. London: Methuen

Chekhov, Michael. *On the Technique of Acting,* 1991. New York: Harper Collins

Cole and Chinoy in Cyril Ives, *Masks and Miracles,* 1995 (dissertation for Master Degree of Education). Exeter: University of Exeter Press

Craig, Edward Gordon in Robert Landy, *The Image of the mask: Implications for Theatre and Therapy, 1985. Journal of Mental Imagery,* 9: 4, pp 43–65

Duchartre, P L. *The Italian Comedy,* 1966. New York: Dover Publications

Gordon, Aonghus and Charlotte Von Bulow, *Practitioner's Guide: How to Apply the Method of Practical Skills in Therapeutic Education,* 2013. Nailsworth: Ruskin Mill Trust

Keirsey, David. *Please Understand Me II,* 1998. Del Mark, California: Prometheus Nemesis Book Company

Lissau, Magda. *The Temperaments and the Arts: Their Relation and Function in Waldorf Pedagogy,* 2003. New York: The Association of Waldorf Schools of North America

Rudlin, John. *Commedia dell' Arte: An Actor's Handbook,* 1994. London: Routledge

Schuré, Edouard. *The Genesis of Tragedy and the Sacred Drama of Eleusis,* 1936. Whitefish, Montana: Kissinger Publishing

Scott, Walter (ed). *Corpus Hermeticum,* 1924. Oxford: Clarendon Press

Steiner, Rudolf. *Speech and Drama,* 1959. London: Anthroposophical Publishing

Steiner, Rudolf. *Awakening to Community,* 1994. New York: Anthroposophic Press, Inc

Steiner, Rudolf. *The Four Temperaments,* 2008. Forest Row: Sophia Books

Steiner, Rudolf. *Freedom and Destiny,* 2009. Forest Row: Rudolf Steiner Press

Throop, Priscilla. *Hildegard von Bingen's Physica,* 1998. Vancouver: Healing Arts Press

Index

Ordering Books

If you have difficulties ordering Hawthorn Press books from a bookshop, you can order direct from our website **www.hawthornpress.com** or the following distributors:

UNITED KINGDOM
BookSource
50 Cambuslang Road, Glasgow
G32 8NB
Tel: (0845) 370 0063
E-mail: orders@booksource.net

AUSTRALIA & NEW ZEALAND
Footprint Books Pty Ltd
4 /8 Jubilee Avenue
Warriewood
NSW 2102
Australia
Tel: (02) 9997 3973
Email: info@footprint.com.au
www.footprint.com.au

USA/NORTH AMERICA
Steiner Books
PO Box 960, Herndon
VA 20172-0960
Tel: (800) 856 8664
Fax: (703) 661 1501
E-mail: service@steinerbooks.org
www.steinerbooks.org

Waldorf Books
Phil & Angela's Company, Inc.
1271 NE Hwy 99W #196
McMinnville, Oregon 97128
Tel: (503) 472-4610
E-mail: info@waldorfbooks.com
www.waldorfbooks.com

Hawthorn Press
www.hawthornpress.com